CLAN-
DESTINY

CLAN-DESTINY

SCOTTISH FAMILYS HISTORICAL JOURNEY TO AMERICA

Bobby V. Johnson

ISBN: 0692826157
ISBN 13: 9780692826157
Library of Congress Control Number: 2017900568
Clan-Destiny, Austin,TEXAS

Aknowledgments

—◆—

THIS BOOK IS DEDICATED TO my father and mother, Zattie May "Jack" Johnson and his wife Katherine Cecil. I will always be proud of their dedication to their church and the way they applied Christian ethics to everyday living. Their lives, love and dedication to family will always be a source of inspiration.

CLAN-DESTINY

—◆—

A Scottish Clan's journey through the numerous changes and challenges in Scotland their journey to the New World and their determination to survive, along with many achievements, failures, hardships and accomplishments.

AUTHOR'S NOTE

———

THE JOHNSON CLAN has its deep roots in Scotland and can be traced back to the twelfth century. They came to America in 1700. We will begin the tracing of this family in the area of their origin and their travels to America in 1700. Their life in America provided many accomplishments, failures, and many times of pride and humiliating defeats. As the history of the Johnson Clan is traced to differing countries of the world, so did the name change slightly to identify with those countries, societies and languages. We will however, trace the Johnsons as they come to America and include the historical facts, as they are known.

Although we will be using facts in most of this story of the Johnson Clan, there are some facts that are unknown or unclear, so we will include in those places and times of uncertainty, what we assume to have happened. We will fill in the areas where some facts are not known so the narrative will be chronological and interesting in content, or where certain information pertaining to those facts is not known in their entirety.

Our study of these times and places in history have given us an insight of the many and various circumstances in history relating to the Gaelic and Scottish land. It is because of the Scottish history that has been written and recorded that make this geographical location and its peoples so unique of all the lands of the world. Some of our historical accounts are compiled from different history sources that are available in numerous historical writings, namely public domain sources, historical accounts and internet sources. We have given credit to those sources in our writing and it is their unique ability to record their thoughts and facts of Scottish history that have assisted us in the following book of Clan Destiny.

TABLE OF CONTENTS

———

THE HISTORY OF SCOTLAND IS humorous at times, yet very complex, disturbing and even exhausting as we look at their numerous conflicts. Most often these conflicts were internal and involved the Gaelic speaking Scots against their neighbors within the land of Scotland. Yet the conflicts were also against their neighboring country to the south. England has tried many times in Scottish history to bring the determined and often stubborn Scots under its subjection and royal rule, but for the most part they always failed until the "Treaty of Union", also known as the "Act of Union", in 1707. In history, there have been some unique ancestral ties with the royalty and their serving a dual role in both Scotland and England that resulted in the King of England also being the King of Scotland and vice versa.

Scotland has experienced extraordinary growth and change throughout its fascinating history yet there have also been decades when the population dramatically declined. What caused this decline? We will cover and share some of those significant moments in Scottish history, including their place in the world. Various tribes and ethnic peoples make the Scottish people a people who have been a proud part of many societies of the world, especially those Scots who came to America in search of a new life. The Johnson clan is only one of many clans with Scottish heritage. The family that we follow through history is now deeply rooted in American society and has been a part of American society since the early seventeen hundreds.

We must first define the term "Clan".

This term comes from the Gaelic word "Clann", meaning offspring or extended family, which relates to common ancestry: a group of families or households, as among the Scottish Highlanders, the heads of which claim descent from a common ancestor. A traditional social unit in the Scottish Highlands, consisting of several families claiming a common ancestor and following the same hereditary chieftain would comprise a clan. There would eventually be over three hundred clans in Scotland. The book entitled <u>Scottish Clans</u> goes to a great extent in explaining the Clan system of Scotland.

Because of the complexity of the Scottish clans, we will first state that there were four distinct Gaelic peoples or tribes within the Scottish clans in their early recorded history. There were numerous Normans and Saxons who were invited to settle in the area of Scotland. They brought with them customs that were not accepted by the Northern Celtics. They wanted to maintain the old customs and traditions of their heritage. This fact alone tended to be a point of contention between the Celtic branch in the "Highlands" (Scottish Gaelic) and that of the "Lowlands" (Scottish-Irish/Old English) or Germanic Anglo Saxon branch.

When Malcolm Canmore, who claims a place in history for the assassination of Macbeth, became king in 1058, the clan system began to form as a system that could be recognized or defined as a clan from its definition. Although there were territorial divisions dating back to the sixth century. Malcolm encouraged the throne of England to adopt the southern form of the English language and abolish the Gaelic form. The English language was adopted as the language of the courts and Roman Catholic became the adopted religion. The adopted religions and denominations would also be a major point of contention for centuries.

As we look at these divisions, we quickly discover that they can, especially in their later years, (after 1000 A.D.) be separated into two distinct classes, those being the Northerners who will become known as the Highlanders and Southerners who are known as the Lowlanders.

This line of separation is mainly a line from the Firth of Clyde in the south west. Edinburg and Glasgow will fall just south of this Firth of the River Forth. More correctly stated, this would be defined as the western and northwestern area being the Highlands and the northeast and south being the lands defined as the Central Lowlands. We can also use as a line of separation, a mountainous chain running in a semi-circle from the River Clyde in the southwest to the north and then northwest to the Moray Firth at the North Sea. Yet we must also realize that the Lowlands will extend north from the border with England, on the eastern side and along the eastern coast with Aberdeen-shire in the north east as being in the Lowlands.

Both western and eastern Scotland is inundated with firths. These are inlets that often stretch several miles inland of which there are many on the western or Highlands side of Scotland. The Highlands are made up of lakes, (better known as lochs) moors and barren hills and are not at all fertile. These lands could only be used for the most part as pasture lands and small garden plots. Much of the thin soil is acidic and much is covered with peat which is normally associated with wet areas and was used by the Scots as a source of heating and cooking. This was a benefit to the Highlanders because of the scarcity of trees and firewood. Many of the hills are rocky and many of the summits are hardly accessible. Needless to say, these areas are less than productive with poor crops and very little vegetation. The western coast is cut up into numerous islets. These islets are often running far inland with the hills dropping straight into the sea.

Even today there are fewer towns in the Highlands. The resulting mindset for the Highlanders because of the difficulty of surviving from the production of the land, was that it was much easier for them to lift or steal the livestock and crops of their neighbors (especially the Lowlanders) than to produce their own. The Highlanders were known for their viciousness, ruthlessness and cunning mentality.

This western and northern land is the area claimed by the Picts in earlier history who were known as a mysterious people. The western and northern settlers came from Ireland which is associated with the Gaelic language, Norway, Sweden and the Scandinavian lands as well as other Gaelic areas. They quickly joined up with the Picts whose origin is uncertain, yet believed to be descendants of the Celts. This was especially notable when the Romans tried to move into these lands and the Romans gave the Gaelic speaking people the name of Caledonians. The Caledonians allied with the Picts in confronting the Roman invaders. It was from these Gaelic speaking people, north of England who had settled in the area north of the Firths that the entire lands were given the name of Scotland.

The Picts had been in Scotland since around 250 A.D. They were regarded as savage warriors. However, the earliest written mention of the Picts occurred in 297 A.D. They were called Picts, probably because of their use of body paint and tattoos. The Picts are also believed to have been descendants of the Celtics, and were well known as fierce fighters. The Romans called the tribes to the north of Hadrian's Wall, the Caledonians, and one Roman writer described them as red haired, large limbed people who were fierce and quick to fight. This was because at the outset of the Roman invasion they quickly went to battle and the Romans determined that they had finally met their match on the battlefield. Their attacks were always accompanied by a hellish yell that would scare even the hardest of any battle-hardened warrior. The Picts and the Caledonians were indeed ruthless warriors as the Romans had determined.

The Picts would eventually begin to fuse with the Gaelics so much that their language would be lost. As a matter of fact, very little is known about the Picts. They would eventually evolve and fuse into the Gaelic world with very little except history to record that they had ever existed. Now their society and the Gaelic society would become as one. Even their history would vanish almost into obscurity.

Although there is evidence of settlements in Scotland as far back as the Stone Age we will begin our historical accounts during the Roman Empire's expansion because this is when the true written history of Scotland begins.

The Romans tried to conquer the highlands but quickly discovered that the vicious Picts and Celts or Caledonians, as they were called by the Romans, were too familiar with their mountainous lands and were vicious in their defense of their lands, for the Romans to ever gain the upper hand. The Highlanders had a dogmatic determination that they were not going allow themselves to be conquered by these invaders of their beloved lands. The Romans eventually remained south of the Forth and Clyde.

The Romans constructed two well-known walls during its occupation of Scotland. One was Hadrian's Wall, which was located near the northern border of England and reached across the entire land from the Tyne in the east to the Solway and/or at the North Sea in the east to the Irish Sea in the west. The Romans took seven years to construct the wall which was painted with white lime mortar and could be seen for miles. This was an attempt by the Romans to quell or alter the numerous raids from the Caledonians. With the construction of this wall the Romans could also control trade coming into and going out of the area and collect taxes on the goods.

The second was Antonin Wall which is located north of Hadrian's Wall and cuts across central Scotland stretching for sixty-three kilometers or 40 miles from the Firth of the River Forth to the Firth of the River Clyde. This wall virtually divided Scotland into two sections but the two walls also divided what was known as Roman lands into three sections. The Roman Empire never succeeded in total occupation or control of Scotland. They were simply unable control or successfully defeat the Caledonians and the Picts. They resigned themselves to occupy the southern lands of Scotland and England south of the Antonin wall.

The Celtic or Gaelic language spoken by the Scots has its origin in Middle Irish. The Scottish Gaelic is not even considered a language by the European Union but is stated as being an indigenous language. The Celts were the first to move into the lands that we know as Scotland, probably coming from Norway to the north east, but certainly from Ireland as well. There was simply too much of the Viking customs in their early history to totally discount Norway as not being part of their ancestry. They were established in the land when history begins to record them, which was at the time of the Roman invasion. This area was as stated earlier divided by the two great Firths or the Rivers, Forth and Clyde and were more Gaelic than British. The Scots, or the other Gaelics in the south were influenced by the English, French and Europeans as well as the Irish.

Because of the continued harassment by the tribes from the north, the Romans eventually decided their expansion into Scotland was not to their benefit and withdrew, toward the south. They first pulled back to Great Britain where they had established a stronghold which they would occupy for several centuries. Today parts of the 63 kilometers (40 miles) long Antonine Wall still stands and is a World Heritage Site.

Many historians agree that the Gaelic speaking people who became known as Scots, probably came from Ireland but were influenced by the Normans and Scandinavian peoples as well.

In early history, the Vikings, who are recognized in history as the world's greatest seamen, began exploits into what are known today as the Scottish lands. The Vikings settled mostly to the west and north of Scotland which placed their settlements in closer proximity to their homeland. They had settled in the Orkney Islands just north of the northern tip of Scotland. The Picts had begun settling the lands in Scotland also and forged a new kingdom called Alba. They were known as pagans.

Later the Christianity that was accepted in the Lowlands spread to the land of Alba and the Picts. The real change came when St. Columba of Ireland moved into the lands and was welcomed to the area and given an islet in the west of Scotland where he quickly brought in twelve monks and settled the area. They built a small church, thereby setting up their missionary work which was completely independent of the Roman Catholic Church.

The lands that we know as Scotland were divided into two different Gaelic speaking peoples with different mindsets and character traits. The Southerners were known as the Saxons or the Lowlanders and were of Germanic influence. Please keep in mind that when we say the Germanic territory of the eleventh and twelfth century, we must realize that it was very different than the country which we recognize as Germany today. The Lowlands are known as the well-watered and fertile lands and were occupied by an industrious and peaceful people who were easy to get along with. These peoples were Christianized by the Romans. One could also say they were civilized by the Romans and were different from the rest of the Celts. This demeanor which was different from their northern relatives resulted from the fact that many of these earlier settlers were Welshmen of Germanic backgrounds and from Ireland as well, although they were greatly influenced by England and France. They were called Saxons, meaning Lowlanders. There are some names accredited to being Scottish that are definitely of Germanic and English influence.

It was in the ninth century that a union took place with the southern Scots and the northern Scots. The union resulted in dramatic changes in the former divisions of Scottish lands and the manner in which the clans conducted themselves.

Calum McNeill makes a strong argument in reference that the "true Scots" are the Highlanders because of the heritage and language which trace back to the Gaelic areas of Ireland.

In the course of history these two different peoples have certainly become mixed if not reversed in their areas of occupation. Nevertheless, they are all now known as Scottish or the lands are known as Scotland. Even the original Gaelic language which was spoken throughout the Scottish lands has now become spoken by only a small percentage of the Scottish population. In the fifteenth century, the Scottish King James was the only King to speak the Gaelic language. He was raised and schooled in the Royal dwellings of his relatives who were royalty in England. Because of his improved education, it was stated that he spoke eight languages. Under the direction of King James, the national language for Scotland was determined to be the Lowlander dialect of the Gaelic language. This was certainly influenced by his close association with the English royalty.

There were, and it seemed that there would always be, wars among the people of Scotland. This included war with the Vikings on several occasions. These were wars to drive them out of the lands of the Scots but there were even occasions when the Vikings would be called on to join the Scots in war against other enemies of the Scottish territory. Then there were the many battles, skirmishes, and wars with the English which went on for centuries. Yet we must not forget the numerous internal battles among the various clans of Scotland itself which claim an interesting place in Scottish history.

The next period of interest was the Macbeth era around 1040 A.D. We are very familiar with the Shakespearean era and

Shakespeare's fictitious writings. The reality is that Macbeth is one of the well-known Scottish kings and ruled the area as the King of Alba from 1040 A.D. until his death in 1057 A.D.

In 1058, after the death of Macbeth, by Malcolm Canmore, Kenneth MacAlpine was recognized as the King of Scotland and was coronated. The place of coronation was on the "Stone of Destiny", which would for centuries be the place of coronation for Scottish royalty. In 1296, King Edward of England realizing the importance of the Stone of Destiny to the Scots, removed the stone and brought it into England where it was called the "Coronation Stone". The red sandstone weighing over 300 pounds, was then used in the coronation of England's royalty and was last used in Queen Elizabeth II's coronation in 1953. The stone remained in Westminster until 1976, when it was returned to Scotland where it is now permanently on display in Edinburg Castle. Malcolm Canmore ushered in a new age for Scotland and the emerging and different distinctions of the many family groups of Scotland which became recognizable as a Clan System.

The Chief or head of the clan was always recognized as the land owner of the clan's lands. The Chief of the clan was the authoritarian and enforced the law. He fined and passed sentence for those who broke the laws of the clan. He had the authority to control all the lands under his clan and it was his responsibility to give portions of the land to the other members according to their size and needs. Yet he retained control and it was his privilege to take back the land and choose an heir (Tanist) who would follow him in the hereditary lineage.

There was a difference in the Scottish Lowlanders and the Gaelic or Highlanders clan system. The Picts and Gaelics felt that the land always belonged to the tribe and they were responsible for its wellbeing with the chief acting only as the father figure of the clan. The Lowlanders clan system recognized the chief as the sole owner of the lands which would always be under his control and had developed as a feudal system. The chief of the clan, or the Lord of the clan controlled and managed the land with those under him being the tenants of the land. Within the overall province of the clan there were divisions of smaller districts. The chief was paid for his protection of the lands, by fines, land rental, portions of the crops produced and for protection. The two differing clan systems would later come together.

One would think that within the overall community each clan member was always ancestrally connected by bloodline or shared the same surname. The definition of "clan" implies this. This was true for many clan members but there were times when other families who had no clan connections, were permitted to join for protection and sanctuary or simply because they had no blood ties or ancestry connection to other clans. When accepted into a clan for whatever reason, they would then receive the same benefits as other clan members but were also accepting the mantle of defending their clan as if they were blood kin. So, a clan could and usually was, made up of several different family groups.

During the times of a feudal war, which was often, the clan took on the form of a military unit. Each clan had its own war cries, its own colors and badges. Each clan member was consulted before joining together with the other clans and going to war. This inclusion had the overall benefit of a continuing spirit of cohesiveness within the individual clan and brought about unity with the combined clans. When going to war, they would do so with a spirit of unity and purpose. Oddly enough, there were also many conflicts between the individual districts within the larger community of clans. These were settled quickly but often led to bloodshed.

CHAPTER 2

━━◆━━

We now proceed to the 1100 A.D. time period which was well known for its feuds and became known as the Feudal Society in history. King William I of Scotland and Henry II of England signed a treaty called "The Treaty of Falsise" in the twelfth century (1174) which ushered in a temporary period of peace in the Scottish lands. In 1189, Richard the Lionheart rescinded the treaty and gave back to Scotland all their rights. He was succeeded by King Alexander I, then his son, King Alexander II, and then by Alexander III.

Under Alexander II, 1214-1249, Scotland realized many great and lasting achievements. During his thirty-five year reign the "Treaty of York" with England was signed which for the first time established the permanent southern border of Scotland. The line was now fixed between the River Tweed and the River Solway. In the view of England, Scotland now existed as a free and independent country. Free of England's ever demanding laws which had previously placed Scotland in subjection to England. More and more land became productive agriculture enterprises which enhanced trade throughout the region and the economy of Scotland flourished. Any agreements or truces between Scotland and England were always short lived.

Because of the complexity and often changing history of Scotland, it would be too extensive to try and include that history in this narrative. We have already mentioned the sometimes-humorous aspects that are a part of the Scottish history. Yet we must also mention that this history is filled with many triumphs and many disasters, as these unique peoples evolved through history. We will resort then to a very brief history of Scotland with additional narratives injected where it is important to mention the historical event in detail. We continue with our chronological narrative in the twelfth century.

In his <u>History of Scotland</u> writings, Tim Lambert included some excellent work on Scotland and the chronology of its history. I am using some excerpts from his writings to aid my narrative in the chronology of events. Some of the wording has been edited, changed or supplemented with additional facts that I felt necessary for clarity.

In the 12th century many towns or boroughs were founded in Scotland and trade flourished. Many of these towns were in the Lowlands although the Highlands continued to thrive also. David the First was the first Scottish king to found mints and to issue his own coins. Scottish kings had very little power. In the west and north, clan Chieftains frequently rebelled against the king during the 12th and 13th centuries. Their devotion to their clan came first above any other clan or appointed kings.

In 1265 the Scottish king conquered the Western Islands, which at that time was ruled by Norway. With the "Treaty of Perth", in 1266, the Norwegian king formally surrendered all his territory in Scotland except for the Orkney and Shetland Islands lying to the north of Scotland.

One night in 1286, Scottish king Alexander III's horse fell in the darkness as he tried to make his way home during a tremendous storm and Alexander was killed. The story is told that Alexander had been away from home for an extended period at Edinburg Castle. He was determined to return home to his beloved wife whose birthday was the next day, even though his journey required him to travel by ferry over a large stretch of water.

He was determined to continue his return despite the dangers. He was advised on several occasions to wait the storm out but he was determined to make it home. As king, he demanded that the ferry operators take him across. When night fell, he continued to ride and became separated from his group. The road led him near some very steep cliffs where his horse apparently strayed near the cliffs and fell. Both he and his horse were killed in the fall.

Alexander III's heir was his little three-year granddaughter, because he had no son to inherit the throne and to whom the throne would pass. The granddaughter was named Margaret. Margaret was known as "The Maid of Norway" and lived in Norway. She died in 1290, on her way to Scotland and was still uncrowned as the Queen of Scotland. She would have been only seven years of age at the time of her death from what was stated to be sea sickness. Margaret was never crowned nor inaugurated. The result was many claimants to the throne. In fact, there were thirteen.

In England, there were some Scottish nobles who had been deprived of their lands in Scotland because they had supported the English. Those nobles now attempted to make John Balliol's son, Edward, king of Scotland. Robert Bruce and John Balliol had very bitter confrontations about who was the legitimate heir to the throne when young Margaret died in 1290. The Scottish nobles in England invaded Scotland by sea and defeated the army that was sent to confront them. The rebels marched to Scone where Edward Balliol was crowned king. He tried to get the support of the English king by promising him Berwick. The Scottish clans frowned on Balliol for his action of giving Scottish lands to the English and he was soon driven out of Scotland.

The Bishop of St Andrews asked Edward I of England to arbitrate. Edward was happy to oblige and he chose John Balliol to be the new king, who was crowned in 1292. Balliol quickly became a puppet of the king of England and fled Scotland to live in exile for several years after Scottish loyalists refused to accept him.

King Edward of England claimed to be overlord of Scotland and he soon made it clear that he wanted Balliol to be a puppet king under his (Edwards) control. Finally, in 1295, Edward tried to force the Scots to join him in a war against France. Balliol rebelled and formed an alliance with France. Then in 1296, Edward invaded Scotland. Balliol was captured and forced to surrender the throne. Edward tried to rule Scotland directly, without a puppet king. He forced many Scottish nobles and landowners to submit to him at Berwick. He then installed English officials to govern Scotland and withdrew.

In 1297 A.D., after the death of Alexander III the British monarch, Edward I, began to look at Scotland as a part of the British Empire and began to march on the Scottish territory to remove the Kings of Scotland and take over the lands as British territory and place Scotland under British rule. When the British marched into Scotland and tried to cross the River Forth and the Sterling Bridge, the Scots were waiting for them. The Scots had the upper hand and drove the British troops into retreat. The results of this battle placed another figure into the Scottish history books. His name was William Wallace.

Sir William Wallace was one of Scotland's most controversial, yet greatest and well known national heroes. Under his leadership, the Scots resistance to English rule and the intrusions into their country finally resulted in Scotland becoming free of English rule, again for a short time.

Wallace was displeased with the aggression of King Edward of England and put together an army consisting of small landowners. He proved himself as a great leader and general at the Battle of Sterling Bridge. Edward's large military force had to cross the River Forth at the narrow bridge, called Sterling. After crossing the Sterling Bridge, there was a narrow road between the hills leading from the bridge and was the only way to escape. Wallace placed his men at the opposite end of the narrow bridge and hidden in the slopes and hills. When Edwards forces entered the bridge, and proceeded to occupy a small area of dry land near the river Wallace began his attack. The only escape was a narrow area between the steep hills that were occupied by Wallace's men or retreat back across the Stirling Bridge. Edward's troops were trapped. The English troops who were not killed or injured quickly broke ranks in a panic and fled in fear. There were several hundred Knights and over three thousand other English footmen who died in the battle.

Edward was not to be defeated and began building an army for the purpose of attacking Scotland and Wallace, and again bringing Scotland into subjugation. Wallace was in the meantime moving to various locations throughout Scotland in hiding. Finally, Edward received word of Wallace's location and began to pursue Wallace. Wallace realized his forces were no match for the large army of Edward who was now leading the English army against him. Wallace continued to avoid contact with Edward, hoping that Edward's army would soon grow weaker from exhaustion in their pursuit and from lack of food.

When near Falkirk, Wallace, knowing that his footmen were no match for the mounted forces of Edward, decided on a plan that may assist his men to overcome his being outnumbered. He drew his men together and placed them in several circles with the spearmen and lancers on the outer fringes of the circle, with the archers in the inner circle. Wallace reportedly told his men "I have brought you to the battle, now show me how well you can fight". Wallace was no match for the English troops and was beaten by the sheer numbers of Edwards troops.

Wallace withdrew and was later captured and sent to London where he was tried for treason. He pleaded that he had never sworn allegiance to Edward; therefore, he was not guilty of treason. He was found guilty and sentenced to death and hanged.

In 1306, Robert the Bruce, who had been crowned king of Scotland, led resistance against the English. The Bruce clan had ancestral ties to Norway. They had migrated from Norway in the eleventh century with William the Conquer, Duke of Norway. The clan first went to England and then to Annandale, Scotland where Robert Bruce became Chief of the Clan. (We will speak more of Robert Bruce later in a unique story which includes the Johnson clan.)

Scottish resistance gradually increased prior to Edward I death in 1307. Then in 1314, the English were utterly defeated at the Battle of Bannockburn. After the battle, Scottish independence was assured. However, it was another fourteen years before the English finally recognized Scottish independence by the Treaty of Northampton in 1328. The English reputation throughout Scottish history was to sign a pledge that the Scottish land was free from English domination, only to again try to bring the lands of Scotland under English subjugation.

The Treaty of Northampton did not bring peace. Robert the Bruce, known as Robert I, died in 1329 and his 5-year-old son became King David II. An unknown disease had troubled Robert I (The Bruce) for several years, and at times became so bad that he was almost totally paralyzed or unable to move. His medical problem was never diagnosed. It was stated that in the end of his life "his tongue was the only thing that moved", as he begged forgiveness for his sometimes cruel and vicious actions. He had been excommunicated from the church because of these actions and was in later years restored yet he continued until death to plead for forgiveness.

There were seven Scottish King Jameses who claimed the throne of Scotland. Some of these kings were also kings of England, serving in a dual role. These were James I, James II, James III, James IV, James V, James VI, and James VII.

In 1503, King James IV of England was married to Margaret Beaufort of England. The marriage had been arranged by her father, King Henry VII. This placed their children in the lineage to also become members of the royalty of England. Margaret became known as Margaret Tudor. She and James IV were fourth cousins. James IV descendant of Robert Bruce became King James IV of Scotland (1488-1513). He restored order to the country of Scotland. His reign was a great age for literature as well as many other accomplishments in Scotland. The first printing press was set up in Edinburgh in 1507 and for the first time in Scotland printing of books and literature was possible. He spoke eight languages and was the last Scottish king to speak the Gaelic language. Aberdeen University was founded in 1495, and in 1496 a law was passed requiring all well-off landowners to send their eldest sons to school for higher education. Usually only the most affluent were the well-educated. A high percentage of the Scots were illiterate. This law changed the level of education for the Scots and they would later claim that a very high percentage was educated.

On August 8, 1503, James IV married Margaret, daughter of Henry VII of England. In 1511 James built a huge warship called the Great Michael. In 1513 he invaded England. The Scots were badly defeated at the battle of Flodden and James himself was killed.

James IV heir, James V, was only a child when his father died and he did not begin to rule Scotland till 1528, fourteen years after his father's death. The Scots again invaded England in 1542 but were defeated at the battle of Solway Moss, in November. The king died in December 1542, while still a young man.

The throne then passed to Mary "Queen of Scots". She was the granddaughter of James IV and Margaret Tudor. Mary was only a baby at that time. Meanwhile, Henry VIII was king of England and wanted his son to wed Mary. The Regent of Scotland, the Earl of Arran signed the Treaty of Greenwich in 1543, agreeing to the child marriage. In December 1543, the Scottish parliament repudiated the treaty. Following this repudiation of the treaty the English invaded southern Scotland 1544 and 1545 and devastated it.

The English invaded Scotland again in 1547 and defeated the Scots at Pinkie. Then again, the English invaded Scotland in 1548, so Mary, Queen of Scots was sent to France for her protection, where she later married into French royalty. Mary was later accused of plotting the death of her cousin, Queen Elizabeth of England.

———◆———

CHAPTER 3

IN THE 16TH CENTURY THE Reformation rocked Scotland, as it had in the rest of Europe. Early in the century, Protestant ideas spread through Scotland and were gradually accepted. Finally, in 1557, a group of Scottish nobles met and signed a covenant to uphold Protestantism.

The leading figure in the Scottish Reformation was John Knox (1505-1572). In 1559, he returned from Geneva where he heard the teachings of John Calvin. Knox's preaching won many converts and in 1560, the Scottish parliament met and severed all links with the Pope. The Parliament also banned the Catholic mass or any doctrine or practice contrary to a confession of faith drawn up by Knox. The Scottish Reformation had succeeded and Scotland was now a Protestant country. The denomination of choice became Presbyterian.

In 1561, Queen Mary returned from France after the death of her husband. Mary remained a devout Catholic but often in secrecy. She was forced to accept the Scottish Reformation but she maintained true to her Catholic religion. Mary married her Catholic cousin Henry Steward, (Lord Darnley) in 1565. Darnley became jealous of Mary's Italian secretary David Riccio. In March 1566, Darnley and his friends murdered Riccio. Mary never forgave Darnley. She then came under the spell of the Earl of Bothwell and fell in love with him.

In 1567, a house where Darnley was staying was blown up. When Darnley's body was found, it was discovered that he had been strangled. Shortly afterwards Mary married the Earl of Bothwell.

Enraged, the Protestant nobles rose up in defiance and captured Mary. They forced her to abdicate in favor of her baby son, who became James VI. She later escaped and raised an army against her enemies, but was defeated at the Battle of Langside. Mary fled to England.

Regents ruled Scotland until James was old enough to rule himself. Mary had claimed that she was also the legitimate Queen of England instead of her cousin Elizabeth, and she was also considered the legitimate sovereign of England by many English Catholics. Mary was accused of plotting to kill her cousin Queen Elizabeth I of England. Mary was arrested and after eighteen years of imprisonment, in 1587, Mary was beheaded in England. In 1589, James married Anne of Denmark. Then in 1603, on the death of Good Queen Bess or Elizabeth I, after her forty-four years of reign, James became King James I of England as well as King James VI of Scotland.

Scottish history includes some very unusual circumstances when it comes to claims to the rights to rule Scotland. Within this history, we find numerous times where Scottish Royalty or claims to the right to rule, and English Royalty are so intertwined through marriage and ancestral ties that it becomes confusing as well as humorous as to who has the legitimate claims to rule in which country. Sometimes the claims were that the individual had dual claims to rule in both countries. This was true of Mary, Queen of Scots claim that she was also the legal heir to the throne of England instead of her cousin Elizabeth.

We also have the rule of King James VI as king of England and Scotland. His accomplishments were many and his intelligence was touted as being responsible for his success. He was taught that

Royalty and the right to rule was a gift from God and he strived to always live up to his God given calling.

One of his greatest accomplishments for which he is recognized in the twenty first century is the translation of the Bible into what we call today "The King James Bible". We know that he was at one time a King of England but we fail to neither realize the century, nor recognize the fact that he served as King of England and King of Scotland in the seventeenth century. The Good King died in 1625.

The Scottish church was different in some of its doctrines and practices from the English Church. The heart of most of the Scottish population was Presbyterian and Protestant while those of England favored the Episcopalian and Catholic religion. Charles I views were said to favor the Catholic religion. Yet history records that Charles I was a devout Episcopalian as was his son after him. James's son, Charles I of England (1625-1649) foolishly tried to bring the Scottish religion in line with the English religion. In 1637 he tried to impose a prayer book on the Scots. The Scots rejected it utterly. On February 28, 1638, a meeting was convened. Two days later nobles and gentlemen in Edinburgh signed a document promising to uphold the "true religion". This document became known as the "National Covenant" and messengers took copies all over Scotland for people to sign as acceptance.

During King Charles I reign, war broke out between the differing religious factions of England and Scotland. In the end the Scottish Presbyterians won. The Scots totally removed every trace of King Charles I involvement from the Church of Scotland and the "Code of the Canons" was thrown out.

Charles I tried to force the Scots to submit to the English and in 1639, he raised an army in England. He was desperately short of money and temporarily made a peace treaty to buy time. In 1640, Charles raised another army but the Scots invaded England and occupied Newcastle and Durham. They withdrew in 1641.

Charles I managed to eliminate two of his major Puritan opponents or tormentors by placing them on the run for their lives. At first the Scots remained neutral, but in 1643 the English parliament persuaded the Scots to join their side by promising to make England Presbyterian. Following this promise in 1644, the Scots sent an army to England.

Not all Scots agreed with this decision. Some supported the king and in 1644, the Marquis of Montrose raised an army in the Highlands to fight for King Charles I. At first Montrose had some successful battles but in 1645, he was defeated at Philiphaugh. Meanwhile the king was defeated in England and in 1646, surrendered to the Scottish army at Newark. Montrose fled to Norway. King Charles I now agreed to make the Presbyterian church prominent in all three kingdoms. This would include Ireland, Scotland and England. Although several promises were made to appease the Scots he remained stubborn even though his life was at stake. He never followed through on his promises. He was king and was therefore given the authority by God, to rule the countries as he saw fit.

The English now dragged their feet about introducing Presbyterianism. When it became clear that they were not going to follow through with their promise, the Scots made a deal with the king. He promised to introduce Presbyterianism in England only for a 3-year trial period. The Scottish army invaded England in 1648, but it was defeated at Preston.

In January 1649, Charles I was tried for high treason and convicted. He was beheaded in January 1649, for his crimes against England. The Scots immediately proclaimed his son Charles II, king. Charles II like his father Charles I and his grandfather James VI was an Episcopalian. He firmly believed that bishops should govern the Church. Nevertheless, to gain the support of the Scots he agreed to accept Presbyterianism in Scotland. In June 1650, he went to Scotland and he was crowned king at Scone in January 1651.

In July 1650, another English army invaded Scotland and occupied Edinburgh. In the summer of 1651 they defeated a Scottish army at Inverkeithing.

A Scottish army then invaded England. They hoped English royalists would join them. They failed to receive the support they were relying on and they were again defeated. The Scots were routed at Worcester in September 1651. Charles II fled abroad.

The English army now occupied the whole of Scotland. The English occupation ended in 1660 when Charles II returned and became king of both England and Scotland.

Charles II restored Episcopalian Bishops to the Church of Scotland and about a third of the ministers resigned. Many Scots, especially in the southwest, held secret religious meetings called conventicles. Gradually the government treated them more harshly. In 1679, the Archbishop of St. Andrews was murdered and unrest spread through the west. The government sent troops to quell the uprising and the Covenanters were defeated at the battle of Bothwell Brig. The Covenanters continued to resist and the government continued to persecute them. The 1680s became known as the "Killing Time".

Charles II died in 1685, and his brother James became King James VII. James VII was a Roman Catholic and both English and Scots feared he would restore Roman Catholicism. James VII was deposed in 1688, and he and his wife fled to France with their son James Francis Edward Stewart. William and Mary became King and Queen of Scotland. The Scottish parliament restored Presbyterianism.

Not all Scots welcomed the new monarchs. The Highlanders rose up under Viscount Dundee. They won a victory at Killiecrankie in 1689, but their leader was killed and the Highlanders dispersed.

The government was determined to bring the Highlands to heel and they ordered the chiefs of all the clans to take an oath of loyalty to King William by the last day of 1691. The chief of the

MacDonalds clan of Glencoe arrived late and took the oath on January 6, 1692. Even though he was only a few days late the government decided to make an example of him. The MacDonalds were one of the largest landholders in Scotland. Because of this fact, they had the distinction of being very powerful. Troops led by Captain Robert Campbell of Glenyon were sent to Glencoe and billeted in cottages there. The MacDonalds treated them hospitably, however, early in the morning of February 13th, Campbell and his men attacked the sleeping MacDonalds. They went from house to house killing the inhabitants and then burning the houses. Altogether thirty-eight people were murdered including the clan chief. This appalling massacre became known as the "Massacre of Glencoe".

King William realized the deposed king; James VII might go to Scotland and claim the Scottish throne. In an effort to prevent this from occurring he urged a union of England and Scotland. The next monarch, Queen Anne, did the same.

Scottish merchants saw economic advantages from a union, and in 1706 the Scots agreed to open negotiations. The Scots wanted a federal union but the English refused. In 1706 another treaty was drawn up but this time with successful progress. The two nations would share a flag and a parliament. Scotland would keep its own church and its own legal system. The Scottish parliament accepted the "Treaty of Union" or "The Act of Union", in 1707. The United Kingdom came into existence on May 1, 1707. England and Scotland now had a treaty to bring the two countries together and put an end to the bitter conflicts that had presented themselves for centuries. Now Ireland was also included and the three countries made up the "United Kingdom" The "Act of Union" would also be known as the "Union of Parliaments" and would now be based in Westminster in London.

The Act of Union was unpopular with many Scots and it soon became even more unpopular. Meanwhile James Francis Edward son of James VII, the king who was deposed in 1688 died in 1701, was determined to regain the throne. His followers were called Jacobites, from the Latin for James, Jacobus. James had many supporters in the Highlands and in 1715, the Earl of Mar proclaimed him king. Lord Mar also denounced the Act of Union.

Now the conflicts would return between the clans of Scotland. Highlanders flocked to join Lord Mar and in September 1715 his forces captured Perth. Still the towns south of the Tay remained loyal to the government.

On November 13, 1715, the Jacobites fought government troops at Sheriffmuir near Dunblane. The battle ended indecisively and afterwards the government army was reinforced. On December 22, 1715, James Edward landed at Peterhead but the government army advanced and the Jacobites withdrew from Perth.

James Francis Edward Stewart, King James III of Scotland, (aka King James VIII of England) was sometimes known as "The Old Pretender", became discouraged and on February 4, 1716, he and Lord Mar left Scotland. The nickname was given because he was said to only be pretending to be the legitimate king when he was not. Afterwards the Jacobite rebellion faded away. The Highlanders were by no means defeated and they remained a threat to the government.

Still the government took some measures to control the Highlands. Fort Augustus was built in 1716 and in 1725-36, General Wade built a network of roads in the Highlands to make it easier for government troops to march from place to place.

James Francis Edward Stewart, King James III, died in 1766, after a reign of sixty-four years. He had fled Scotland and died in Rome.

His son Charles Edward Stewart, became king. He was also known as "Bonnie Prince Charles" and was also known as "The Young Pretender". He became king and is remembered for his unsuccessful support of the continued "Jacobite Uprising". He attempted to restore his family to the throne of Great Britain. His attempt failed when he was defeated at the battle of Culloden. He died in 1788.

CHAPTER 4

—————

AS WE HAVE LOOKED AT this brief history of Scotland from the 1000 A.D. time period, through the mid seventeen hundreds, we realize the numerous conflicts that occurred between England and the Scots as well as other countries near England. We can understand the desire, by many, to leave Scotland and the area that seemed to be in constant turmoil. In the fourteen hundreds, (fifteenth century) the population of Scotland declined dramatically because of all the Clan wars, the continuous conflicts with England and the continuous turmoil that was forever present in the lives of all the population.

No wonder there were so many people who were willing to forsake their lifestyles in the old country for the possibility of improvement in their futures in a new land that had just begun to be explored and settled. That new land was the Americas. We intentionally took this brief history trip up through the early to mid-seventeen hundreds because this is the time when one of the Johnsons in our ancestral lineage made his way to America. As our narrative continues with the Johnson Clan, we will also bring in additional history of Scotland as it relates to that period of Johnson history.

We must understand that war was not just with the British but among the many clans in Scotland as well. War between the clans was always on the fringe of the inevitable. Only a small spark could once again incite still another incident, however small it may seem to the outsider. It may have been a stolen pig, a political dispute, another clan infringing on the property boundaries or something so non-incidental as spoken words that were perhaps intended to be an insult or perhaps taken out of context and mistakenly heard as an insult.

Feuds were always a part of life for the Johnston Clan of the Lowlands and had been for about six hundred years as they strived to hold on to their part of the Scottish territory that they claimed in Eastern Lothian. This territory is in the area of Edinburgh. They were always vigilant in case the English Freebooters decided to show up unexpectedly. These were English bandits and pirates or thugs who would show up and steal the possessions of the Scot's and seemed to be encouraged by the English rulers. It seemed that these intrusions were almost always carried out on the clans in the Lowlands. Perhaps there was such a dreaded fear of the Highlands clans that they tried to avoid that area. Most likely it was due to the fact that the Highlanders were always in a struggle for their own survival. The Highlanders were often responsible for intrusions and theft on the clans of the Lowlands.

Then there were always skirmishes and feuds with their neighbors. Some were wealthy and powerful with large possessions of property. There were the MacDonalds, the Crichtons of Sanquhar and the Maxwells of Nitsdale who were always a threat as they continued to try to add to their wealth and land possessions. There were other large landholders also. Some of these were the Bruces, the Comwyns and the Kirkpatricks and the Johnstons. These feuds were commonplace not only in Scotland but were equally prevalent in England, Wales and Ireland.

The English were constantly trying to exercise their influence on the smaller countries and trying to evoke fear as they endeavored to gain more control and influence on the inhabitants of the smaller countries. England was after all a country with great pride in, not only its power as a country, but also took enormous pride in its form of government, the constitutional monarchy. The King of England was in control, had always been and always would be. He was the authority and what he said was the rule of the land. These smaller countries, which had their own declared rulers or chiefs and refused to adhere to the English king's authority, were a thorn in the side of English royalty and could not be tolerated nor permitted to continue.

The Johnston Clan dates to Stiven "The Clerk" Johnston of Caskieben (founder of the family in Aberdeen-shire, Scotland) and his son, Sir John De Johnston (proprietor of the lands of Ballindalloch). He was first of record and noted as the Lord of Annandale. Annandale and the County of Dumfries are located in the southern Lowlands and join borders with England. The Johnston clan was territorial and they too were known not only as Barons and Lords in the Scottish territory but a powerful clan to be reckoned with.

Some of the first recorded history of the Johnstons was in 1194 when John Johnstone swore fealty to Edward King of England. Sir John Johnstone was Knight of the county of Dumfries. He was awarded a grant of land near Threave Castle, which had originally been a part of the Douglas lands of Galloway. The Johnstons were known only to raid the lands of the English to the south, however it was also known that a bitter feud existed between the Johnston's and the Maxwells. The Maxwells were a powerful clan and supported Robert the Bruce in the battle of Bannockburn as did the Johnstons.

Many years later the feud still existed between the Maxwell's and the Johnstons. An ancestor of John Johnstone, John De Johnstone, was later shot in the back by his bitter enemy, the ninth Lord Maxwell. Maxwell was charged with the murder and hanged in 1614.

The Johnstons also had a long-standing feud with the Clan Moffat and the Clan Douglass. In fourteen forty-eight the king awarded the lands of the Douglass clan to the Johnstons for their support in an uprising of the Douglass's against the King.

The Johnstons' feud with the Clan Moffat (another Scottish border clan) came to a head in the mid fifteen hundreds. In fifteen fifty-seven the feud climaxed in the murder of the Moffat Chief, Robert Moffat. The Johnstons went on the rampage and then burned the local church where many of the ranking and important members of the Moffat clan were hiding. The church burned with all the occupants perishing. Those who attempted escape were slaughtered by the Johnston clan. The Moffat Clan was almost totally wiped out. Seventy years later the lands owned by the Moffats, were given to the Johnston clan because the Moffat clan could no longer pay their massive debts.

Please be aware that this type of uprising against another clan was not exclusive to the Johnston clan. There were continual bitter feuds between tribes and clans that resulted in many deaths. There were disputes, which always led to verbal conflicts and confrontations, injury and even death. This was the way of the early Scottish clans. After all, one had to protect his meager possessions or his property, the clan's family name or one's honor. No one was permitted to insult the members of the family clan even if the words or the actions were correct or justified. After all what was justification? Was it only a word that had somehow been deemed a part of the vocabulary? Was justification really the action of showing something to be right or reasonable? If so, then the clan was indeed justified in its action or its reaction to another unjustified provocation by other clans. Especially when they went against the family honor or tried to encroach on the clan's declared territory.

So, it was with the Johnson clan of Scotland. **"Never Unprepared or Always Ready." "Aye Always Ready".** It was in the Johnson coat of arms and a part of the emblem or shield. It was there for all who desired to look at the Coat of Arms and to try and identify or understand the meaning of the symbols, colors, and motto. Each component had meaning and was a part of the Coat of Arms for a purpose. Everyone could readily see and understand that the Johnson Clan was also as important as the many other clans in Scotland and the Coat of Arms with all its colors designs and inscriptions indicated the pride that the Johnsons felt. Yes! They were as important and equally proud as any of the many clans of Scotland.

The Johnston clan was one of the most powerful clans of Scotland and the Lowlands. They had extensive land holdings and for over six hundred years held those lands. They were near the border of their southern neighbor, England and were always on watch for intrusions by the English royalty and their armies and the Freebooters.

There was one thing that perhaps differentiated the Johnston Clan from the other clans in Scotland, and this difference was recognized by all. They stood their ground and would defend their clan and their territory at the slightest provocation. This trait was always recognized by the other clans and respected by the other clans.

Going back to the thirteenth century, there was evidence that the Johnston Clan would also involve itself into situations that they believed in, and they were even caught up in disputes in which they could have or should have remained distant.

Perhaps arguably so, was the case of Sir Roberet Bruce around 1274. When Sir Roberet Bruce, who would later be recognized or known as King Roberet of Scotland, or King Robert I, was fighting Comwyn for the throne of Scotland, each of the men were always accompanied by a few followers. Bruce contended that he was next in line to the throne, and this was contested by two others who also felt that the throne was rightfully theirs to claim. On this particular occasion, they met at a church in Dumfries, Scotland, one Sunday to discuss their differences of opinion concerning some of those issues. They were meeting there with other well-known Scots who were involved in the politics of the time and each man had supporters present. Among those who were meeting at the church were Lord Kirkpatrick and Lord Johnston. As the political discussions ensued and the tempers became inflamed, each man tried to confront the other with their political positions and views, as to where Scotland was to be led and who was to lead Scotland in the future. Tempers continued to become inflamed to the point of physical confrontations. A melee broke out among the men meeting at the church. Roberet Bruce pulled a knife and stabbed Comwyn who then fell to the church floor bleeding profusely.

Comwyn's men outnumbered Bruce's men and so they ran for their horses. As they mounted their horses to run for cover, Bruce made the remark that he "wondered if I killed Comwyn or just injured him". Lord Kirkpatrick immediately dismounted and ran over to Lord Johnston asking if Lord Johnston had a dagger on him. Lord Johnston immediately replied **"NEVER UNPREPARED, AYE ALWAYS READY ALWAYS READY"** and handed Kirkpatrick his dagger.

Lord Kirkpatrick then ran back into the church and in all the confusion stabbed Comwyn again, this time fatally. As he made his way back to his companions and mounted his horse for the getaway, he was quoted as saying **"I make sure men, I make sure"**. The then dead Comwyn's, followers quickly pursued Roberet Bruce and his followers. Bruce and his men escaped and were forced to hide. They resigned themselves to sleeping in the forests and woods for the next three days and nights. Bruce would later state that he and his companions were forced to sleep in the forests **"wi't nae a pillow for our heads"**.

When Roberet Bruce was later (in 1306) confirmed to the Scottish throne, where he served until his death in 1329, he added to the coat of arms of those followers who had assisted him. These additions included the John De Johnston clan and the Kirkpatrick clan's Coat of Arms. It included the Silver Shield and the Black Cross. King Roberet Bruce then granted upon each of the men, Three Golden Pillows, which denoted the three nights they spent hiding in the forests and woods. Bruce then added the saying by Johnston at the church **"Always Ready, Aye Always Ready"**, to Johnston's coat of arms. Then to Lord Johnston he also added the "Winged Spur", denoting the flight after Comwyn's death by stabbing; with Johnston's dagger. To Kirkpatrick's shield he added or granted the "Mailed Hand" grasping the bloody dagger. Such was the chivalry even in the thirteenth century.

After Comwyn's death, Robert the Bruce went after the Comwyn's people with a vengeance. He attacked the occupants of the land killing and utterly destroying all the homes and dwellings in the area. Robert became known as a vicious and a merciless killer of men, women and children. He was excommunicated from the church on at least two occasions. When he was near death he was restored to the church but would constantly state how he had needlessly taken innocent blood and pleaded for forgiveness. Yet after his death and despite his vicious and murderous past, Robert I, or "Robert the Bruce", was remembered by the construction of a large stone statue commemorating his leadership over Scotland.

So how did the Johnston clan's name evolve to the Johnson name that continues to this day? Historians differ on this derivation. Some declare that, as was common in the Eastern Highlands of "Dear Auld Scotland", the name often evolved as a corruption of the original name. Webster defines this as: "dishonest or fraudulent conduct by those in power, typically involving bribery; the process by which something, typically a word or expression, is changed from its original use or meaning to one that is regarded as erroneous or debased". Thus, corruption of the Celtic name, "Mac" or "Son of Shame", becomes McShame or McShane. Then there was the name of Steward becoming Stewart - or perhaps Celtic for John or the "Son of John" becoming Johnson.

Then others state that the family simply took its name from a great stone or rock near the clan's family seat near the area of Annandale in Scotland.

Stones or large rocks were always an important symbol in Scottish history. "The Stone of Destiny" is one of the most familiar. This stone was where the Scottish King was inaugurated until it was taken by England in one of their many battles. It was not returned to Scotland until 1976. Thus, the name of "John-stone" with the E left off would become Johnston. It was common for names to be changed slightly over the centuries. Most of those changes were simply to change a letter or drop a letter from the name. There were many changes or adaptations of numerous families over the centuries and it often was influenced by the country in which they lived.

As some family lineages are traced we find many changes such as the name Johnston becoming Johnson. Another family name change was that of the English name of "Hosbandgh" evolving into a change upon their arrival in America of "Husbands". Either or all of these changes have an equal foundation for correctness.

Throughout history the Johnson name has been identified with such positions as: Marquises of Annandale, Dukes of Annandale, Dukes of Chaskichbere, Earls of Annandale, Barons Johnston and Viscounts Chifden.

There has been in the history of the Johnson clan, at least eight Baronets and four lines of Barons. They have been Marquises of Lithgow and Knighthoods of Johnsons, with the Knighthoods of Johnsons being numerous. Even in history of recent past there have been descendants of the Johnson clan who have been "Medal of Honor" recipients, Presidents and leaders, as well as "Space Shuttle Pilots".

Thus, we have some of the Johnson history from the clan's origins in the area of Annandale, Scotland but what about the history of the Johnson clan as they migrated away from Scotland to other places of the world.

CHAPTER 5

———

As TIME, EXTENDED AND FAMILIES within the clan continued to grow the lands belonging to the clans, continued to be divided up to meet the needs of the growing population within. Acquisition of additional lands was impossible without a clan war. The land owned by clan members continued to dwindle amidst the growing family demands until it became extremely difficult to live and provide for one's family. The land plots became smaller and smaller. Instead of the clans becoming wealthier, they, in most cases continued to slowly sink into the meager existence of poverty with only the elite of the clan becoming wealthy. Only the more influential and powerful members of the clan lived a seemingly unchallenged lifestyle. But not everyone could be Barons or Lords or influenced by the upper ruling class.

Something had to change for the clan members and the change would only come about through change of location. From the demands of survival, or the continued conflicts within the clans and the neighboring clans or the centuries long conflicts with their southern neighbor, the country of England, there was an ever-increasing need or desire to separate from the area of their difficulties. The clan members slowly began to migrate to the despised England, perhaps because many identified and/or supported the leadership of England or perhaps for protection. Some began to migrate to Ireland and to the territories nearer to their beloved

Scotland. These territories of migration were influenced first by the possibility of obtaining land for the family, or by political means or by social acceptance within the desired areas of migration. There would always be a deep love for their beloved Scotland regardless of where in the world they were to reside.

By the late 1500s and early 1600s, the Scottish people were even migrating to west Europe. Then at the turn of the century came the continued rumor of the new land of America. Individuals were encouraged to make the voyage so they could get away from the oppression of England and the Church of England with its religious demands and begin a new life in what would become known as the "New World". Some were forced to leave or flee their lands because of crimes or statements against the royalty and rulers of England. England had developed a policy of often charging individuals with petty crimes and then forcing them to be shipped to the new world as punishment. This was the English policy concerning the Scots and even Englishmen who had fallen out of favor with their countries royalty.

As we have seen in the brief history, religious conflicts and divisions caused from differences in religious philosophy were many. There were the Catholics, the Protestants, or the Anglicans and the Presbyterians. The land in the New World was vast. Also, the possibilities and desire for freedom, which included religious freedom, were the encouraging factors. It was correctly perceived that the early colonies would face a difficult time and many hardships could be expected. Even with these mentioned difficulties, many decided the perceived difficulties could be accepted and overcome when freedom for themselves, religious freedom and land acquisition were the main attractions.

CHAPTER 6

WE WILL FIRST LOOK AT the adventures of three young Johnson men and their departure from the old countries. Then we will trace their lives in America and their descendants. From there we will follow one specific Johnson family through their struggles, adventures, accomplishments, hardships, moments of pride and their moments of humiliation and shame.

First, we find Nicolas Johnson, a young Scottish lad who desired adventure. He was young and had not married so he was continuously reminded of the adventure of leaving Scotland and traveling to the New World called America, which was claimed by England, France and Spain. Although in the eastern portion of America there were deep ties to England, there was reason to believe that the life in America would be an improvement over the struggles he and his family had faced for generations. One of the problems that had existed between the English and the Scots was that of religion. The Church of England was controlled by the King of England. The church had forced their religious beliefs and restrictions on their people for many years. Most if not all of those individuals and families who were making passage to the new world, were doing so in the desire for religious freedom.

As much as he despised England and their continuous threats and their desires to totally control his beloved Scotland, Nicolas

Johnson began to feel that he would be better off to be far removed from the realistic threats that England presented to the countries around Scotland. Perhaps, just perhaps, he could find passage on one of the sailing ships that were now making voyages to America.

At last he made up his mind to leave the Johnson clan and his Scottish land and seek voyage to America. He could work as a ship's mate for passage and with his meager saving and belongings, perhaps he could meet the requirements to be accepted as one of the settlers going to America. When there, he would possibly meet one of the new immigrants, marry and begin a family where the possibilities of land ownership and becoming influential and even wealthy were a realistic possibility. The Scottish work ethics were always a benefit and would prove to be an advantage in the New World of America.

One of the earlier voyages to America was organized in 1590 and 113 settlers signed up to go to the New Country. John White who would be the appointed governor of the new colony to be located at Roanoke Island, was charged with the solicitation of early colonists for this voyage. John White was second in command of the ship that would take this early group of pilgrims to America. An earlier settlement had been attempted in this same area by the famous Sir Walter Raleigh in the 1580s, however this attempted settlement failed. Among the colonists for the voyage was John White's daughter, Elinor Dare who would give birth to the first white child born in the new colony and in America.

Also on the manifest was one, Nicholas Johnson from Scotland.

one voice requested him to return himself into England for the
better and sooner of obtaining supplies and other necessaries for
them; but he refused it, and alledged many sufficient causes why
he would not. . . . Also he alledged, that seeing they intended to
remove fifty miles further up into the main presently, he being then
absent, his stuff and goods might be both spoiled, and most of them
pilfered away in the carriage. . . .

[Eventually White was persuaded to return to England. On
the seventh and twentieth of August the admiral and the fly-boat
weighed anchor and set sail for England, where they arrived in
November. The pinnace remained in the sound.]

The names of all the men, women and children which safely
arrived in Virginia and remained to inhabit there 1587.

John White	John Bright	Hugh Pattenson
Roger Bailey	William Dutton	Martin Sutton
Ananias Dare	Maurice Allen	John Farre
Chrystopher Cooper	William Waters	John Bridger
Thomas Stevens	Richard Arthur	Griffin Jones
John Sampson	John Chapman	Richard Shabedge
Clement Taylor	William Clement	James Lasie
William Sole	Robert Little	John Cheven
John Cotsmur	Hugh Tayler	Thomas Hewet
Humphrey Newton	Hugh Wildye	William Berde
Thomas Colman	Lewes Wotton	Henry Brown
Thomas Gramme	Michael Bishop	Richard Tompkins
Thomas Butler	Henry Rufoote	Charles Florrie
Edward Powell	Henry Dorrell	Henry Payne
John Burdon	Henry Mylton	William Nichols
James Hinde	Thomas Harris	John Borden
Thomas Ellis	Thomas Phevens	Michael Myllet
William Browne	Mark Bennett	Thomas Smith
Dionys. Harvie	John Gibbes	Richard Kemme
Roger Pratt	John Stillman	Thomas Harris
George Howe	Robert Wilkinson	Richard Taverner
Simon Fernando	John Tydway	John Earnest
Nicholas Johnson	Ambrose Viccars	Henry Johnson
Thomas Warner	Edmund English	John Starte
Anthony Cage	Thomas Topan	Richard Darige
John Jones	Henry Berry	William Lucas
William Willes	Richard Berry	Arnold Archand
John Brooke	John Spendlove	John Wright
Cuthbert White	John Hemington	Thomas Scott

The colonists were settled in Roanoke Island in present day North Carolina. After the settlement was begun and construction of the small colony was nearly complete, supplies began to run low. Fearing that they may have a difficult time in these early stages of their settlement of producing enough food for the settlers and certainly there was a need to increase all the main staples, a plan of action was agreed upon. When supplies began to run low it was agreed that John White, because of his connections, would make a return voyage back to England to obtain supplies for the struggling colony.

When he arrived in England, a situation had developed that would delay his return to the New World. A war with Spain had broken out and White could not immediately obtain a ship to carry his supplies back to the New World and his Roanoke Island colony. White was successful in finally acquiring two small vessels to carry his supplies. On the outward voyage the two ships captains decided to attack some Spanish vessels. Their theory was that they could overwhelm the Spanish vessels and enhance their wealth by stealing the supplies of the Spanish vessels. They were not prepared for the outcome. They lost in their privateering venture attack and as a result the Spanish vessels were successful in taking all the supplies from the two vessels that were intended for White's Roanoke Settlement. John White then returned to England. This resulted in a three-year delay before the return voyage could be arranged.

White was eventually successful in returning to Roanoke Island in 1593, which was three years after leaving the 113 colonists. He had planned an expected quick voyage to England for supplies and then a rapid return with those supplies that the colonist so desperately needed. The colonists eagerly awaited his return.

When he finally made his way back to the Island and the area where the settlers had constructed their settlement, there were fires seen through the trees but there were no colonists to be found. There were indications of previous fires in now rotted trees and some letters carved in the timbers of the settlement that spelled out CROATOAN. An agreed upon signal to indicate distress had been determined to be the letters CRO, but was also be overlaid by a specific cross design. The letters found were not overlaid with the cross so White believed that the settlers had simply moved about fifty miles away to the area known as Croatians. He believed that they had not left the original area because of stress or possible attacks from the Native Indians in the area. It was also discovered that the settlement had been dismantled, therefore dispelling any ideas that the settlement had been attacked but had instead been intentionally dismantled and moved. After a search, weather conditions changed and the ship's captains refused to delay any longer to permit White to search for his now missing colony. They hurriedly left the settlement area ahead of the approaching storms. John White and his group were never able to locate the colonists, who would become known as the "Lost Colonists". One theory has it that they were taken into the Indian tribe of Croatans and this was the intention of the message carved into the timbers. John White returned to England and never heard of his daughter and granddaughter whom he had left on the Roanoke Island as members of the early colony.

There were over the next several decades, reports of seeing mixed Indian people with blond hair, gray or green eyes, and some English-speaking Indians. There would later in history be a discovery of a group of people who were called Melunigans. These people spoke with a Portuguese accent and dialect and were obviously not Native Indians and they refused to assimilate into the Indian culture. It was later determined through various means, that they were indeed of Portuguese ancestry. After much debate over the information obtained from these people, it was determined that they had to be of European descent. Present day DNA has confirmed their Portuguese ancestry. The "Moors Sundry Act" was passed in 1790, as a direct result of the discovery of these people in America. The South Carolina Legislature gave special status to those of Moroccan descent in the state.

Of the group of settlers brought to America by John White, there were individuals from Portugal who had been in their history, refugees from the Spanish Inquisition of 1492 and its edict issued by the king of Spain that all peoples living in Spain would become Catholics and profess allegiance to Spain and the Catholic religion. Anyone who would not, would be forced to leave Spain within fourteen days or be imprisoned or killed. The resulting exodus included large numbers of Jewish people and Muslims. There were in Spain at this time a large number of people known as the Moors. John White had intentionally encouraged some these people to be a part of his expedition under the pretext that he would take them to Morocco. There were in fact names adopted by the Cherokee Indians that were of Arabic origin and also the multiuse of the word "Allah" in the language of the Indians as well as English words.

With this information, it can be concluded that indeed some of those colonists of the John White settlement on Roanoke Island, did indeed survive to become known as the Melunigans. Others also concluded that these were possibly a part of another expedition who had become separated from their original colony and banded together in the new settlement. However, there was never any conclusive evidence as to the fate or the survival of the colony. They would become known in the annals of history as "The Lost Colony".

Was the Nicolas Johnson mentioned earlier as a part of the John White expedition, the first Johnson to arrive in America? We cannot prove that he was the first but he was certainly one of only a couple of Johnsons to enter the American settlements. Nor can we prove that he survived with a later group who was discovered in the area where the original Roanoke colony was settled. Nicolas Johnson was indeed a Scottish young lad who had left his life in Scotland to become one of the first settlers in the New World.

In the lists of colonists some 20 years later who had settled in Jamestown, Williamsburg and surrounding colonies, there are several Johnsons mentioned. As we look at the early history and the early settlers arriving in the "New World" we will see that by the early 1600s there are several Johnsons who are listed in the settlement areas.

King James VI was king of Scotland in 1587. He also became the declared King of England as King James I, in 1603, serving a dual role. He is accredited with one of the world's greatest publications and the world's best-selling version of the Bible. In sixteen eleven the first translation of the Bible was completed and became known as the King James Version.

CHAPTER 7

———————

IN 1618, THE JAMESTOWN COLONY of Virginia had an abundance of land but very few people. They needed workers for the growing of tobacco, which had become the most important crop for the colony's economy. The key to encouraging others to migrate from Europe to America was the inclusion of being able to obtain large plats of land. This would also require large numbers of people to work the land and the crops.

To alleviate the labor shortage, governors started a system called "headrighting". Headright simply means the right per head and in this setting it is a legal right to a grant of land. It was generally offered to settlers who were planning to occupy uninhabited areas. Ownership of land was unheard of in England for the poor and lower classes. The headright system established the granting of a fifty-acre patent of land to anyone who paid for his or another's passage across the Atlantic. A patent is any official document securing a right to portions of unsettled land. An individual could pay for the passage of his wife or any other family member or a friend or an associate. The individual who paid for the passage of another became known as the "patentee" and received fifty acres of land for each individual for whom he had paid their fare. The result was that many of these wealthy payees also became large land holders in America as they not only paid for their family members but others as well. The result was that they could then claim additional portions of land.

In many instances, the person for whom passage was paid, bore an obligation to work off his debt once he arrived in the new world. He would then become an indentured servant. If he was a skilled tradesman, he often worked up to five years to pay off the average six pounds paid for his passage. If he was unskilled, he generally worked up to seven years to pay off his passage.

The headright system was used in other colonies, but only in Virginia have the records significantly helped researchers find ancestors. However, we did also come across copies of reports of headrights at the archives and information services division at the Texas State Library. This collection of eighteen boxes of "Headright" reports from many of the counties of Texas from 1836 to 1855, is available for study.

In Virginia, few ship records have survived, leaving only the headright records to imply successful passage was made to the new world. One bonus is that, if you can find out where in England the patentee (the one who paid for the passage) lived, you can possibly narrow your search for the person for whom he paid passage, as they sometimes lived in or around the same geographical area. All social classes, including "gentry" can sometimes be located. **Gentry:** upper or ruling class; aristocracy, a class whose members are entitled to bear a coat of arms though not of noble rank; *especially*: The landed proprietors having such gentry status had headrights.[1]

Often, they were the second or third sons of a "gentry's" family. It was incorrectly believed that ship captains paid a majority of passages. Although this is incorrect, the captains did often work in conjunction with wealthy individuals who were trying to acquire more people to migrate to America. For his efforts, the Captain would receive a bonus from the payor for his efforts. This would

---

1 Webster's Dictionary

guarantee the wealthy more acquisition of the available land and individuals to work on the land until passage was paid.

As was common, when one paid the passage for an individual, the recipient of the paid passage then became indebted or indentured to the payor for an agreed upon period of time or until the passage was paid. This was one of the solutions to the labor problems faced by the early landowners who were involved in the labor-intensive tobacco growing. These indentured workers were often used in the fields where the tobacco and cotton were grown until their debts were paid. Women or spouses of the men were also indentured to become laborers but their duties were normally in the homes or businesses of the payor although it was not uncommon for women to work alongside their husbands or other men, in the fields or assisting with tobacco harvesting or in the curing barns.

Even the tobacco growing in America influenced the lands and people of Scotland. The trade of tobacco made many Scots wealthy. There were some of the Scots who owned their own ships to first transport goods to America and make the return voyage with a ship load of tobacco straight to the Scottish ports to be distributed. In the late seventeen hundreds, one of the largest estates ever constructed in Scotland was owned by one of the Big Three Tobacco Lords of Scotland.

We can see how this system of obtaining laborers for the larger farms evolved. As the number of indentured laborers became fewer and the farms continued to grow larger with the now profitable crops of cotton and tobacco, the laborers required were more numerous but the number of indentured servants was dwindling.

Although slavery was not new to the world and had been in practice almost as long as the population of the world., it began to find its way into the population of the Americas. First of course, slaves were taken to the Islands of Puerto Rica, Dominican, Jamaica, Cuba and other of the Caribbean lands. Workers were needed there for the growing sugar cane fields. Then the slavery ideas came to America. Especially to the crop growing regions of the south, where tobacco farming and cotton farming were growing as the demand for these crops were expanding worldwide.

We need not fool ourselves into thinking that slavery was exclusively in the south. Not so! Indentured servants and slavery was also prevalent in the north, just not on the scale that it was in the islands and the southern states.

———

CHAPTER 8

IN 1611 A WILLIAM JOHNSON who was listed as a laborer for trade was in the Jamestown colony. Then in 1618 another William Johnson who was listed as a refiner resided there. We mention the William Johnsons intentionally because as we search the records to trace our ancestors it becomes evident that we are descended from a William Johnson in the early 1700s.

There are also mentioned a John Johnson, as well as two Johnson children who are listed as orphans. At this point in time we are aware that there are two William Johnsons. One was a laborer who came on the first ship into Jamestown and William Johnson, a refiner on the first supply ship into the Colonies. Then there is John Johnson of the New Colony in 1618. But the real question becomes whose family members or nieces/ nephews are these orphans that are mentioned? It is unknown as to who their parents were. Perhaps they were orphaned during the sometimes-treacherous voyage to America. History records indicate that there were many deaths from disease, illness and other incidents that plagued the early colonists. This also included those lost during the voyage.

The genealogy line cannot be traced in exactness for our side of the Johnson clan. We can only continue to study records and trace records and documents to try and make the connection. We know that our ancestor Zachariah Johnson was in Edgefield District, South Carolina in 1756 because he had three sons born and listed in records as being born in Edgefield District, S.C. Edgefield District was in the eastern side of South Carolina and would later be known as Edgefield County, South Carolina, as the settlements grew and statehood was declared. What we cannot discern is where Zachariah lived prior to journeying to Edgefield District. What his life prior to South Carolina beheld, we may never know. Had his parents immigrated to America through Charleston or were they a part of those increasing numbers landing in Virginia. This is what we will try desperately to clarify as we journey through this difficult task of tracing our ancestors.

Let us first follow another Johnson of Scottish decent who was born and christened, Zachariah Johnson. Edward Johnson was born in Ireland in 1675. In early history, many Johnsons had migrated to Ireland from their origin in the Norwegian area of northwest Europe, but they then migrated to Scotland. They would later begin to leave Scotland for other countries to try and escape the stressful life in Scotland. This area on the English/Scottish border was known for its border wars and the Johnson Clan in its early history was known, as were other clans, as a warrior clan.

As we study the history of this area of Annandale and Dumfries in the south and southeast area of Scotland, we are immediately impressed by its landscape and its beauty. The brilliant green, rolling or inundating hills are amazing to look upon. The countryside is spectacular in its photogenic appeal.

Edward Johnson made his way from the place of his birth in Ireland to the Annandale, Scotland area around 1690-1695 where he married and had one son whom they named William. William was born in Dumfries-shire, Scotland in 1697. Edwards's wife's name is unknown.

At an early age, William was an adventurous young man and it is known that as more and more individuals from the Scottish, Irish and English areas were leaving to become colonists in America, William began to anticipate the time when he would be of age and could join in the excitement of leaving Annandale and going to America. He obtained voyage and landed in Virginia around 1720, taking up residence in Port Royal, Virginia.

William met and married Nancy Ann Chew on October 12, 1723 in Spotsylvania, Virginia. He and Nancy Ann had several children in their nineteen years of marriage. Nancy Ann Chew's parents were Captain Larkin Chew and Hannah Roy of Virginia, of mixed Indian heritage. Nancy Ann Chew Johnson died in 1742.

Two years later William married a widow named Elizabeth Wyatt in Spotsylvania, Virginia. Elizabeth Wyatt was born in 1705 in Gloucester, Virginia. Records show that a son named Zachariah Johnson was born to them in 1743 in Augusta County, Virginia. Elizabeth Wyatt died in 1756 in Virginia and William then married Betty Taylor. William's son, Zachariah Johnson died in 1800 in Augusta, Virginia and probably lived his entire life in this area. So, we now must remove him from the possibility of our ancestral heritage because of several facts already known which do not fit in with the known facts of the Johnson history.

Yet, as we follow this Zachariah Johnson you will notice also that the birth date is in 1743. However other information, although never conclusive, indicated that our Zachariah was born around 1740. There is no possibility that this Zachariah was born in Edgefield District, S.C. because records indicate that this Zachariah was in Virginia all his life.

Records seem to indicate that his father William and his mother Elizabeth Wyatt were always around the Spotsylvania, Virginia area. The information that our Zachariah Johnson was born in Edgefield District, S.C. has always been inconclusive and was based more on a guess rather than factual information. Even his birth date was followed with a question mark indicating that the exact date was only a guess with neither his place of death nor the year of his death being known.

———◆———

CHAPTER 9

WE WILL NOW FOLLOW ANOTHER line of Johnsons and another Zachariah Johnson. This Zachariah Johnson was born in Ireland in 1740 and was of Scottish descent. This Zachariah made his way to America while still in his teens and indeed made his way to South Carolina, married and began a family there. There are some who have worked diligently on tracing our Johnson ancestry and have made this connection by speculation. They have therefore connected one son Shadrach, to this Zachariah Johnson because there was also a Shadrach in our lineage. However, our Zachariah had three sons being born. These sons were William born in 1756, Shadrach who was born in 1759, and a third son Jeremiah born in 1761.We will follow Jeremiah Johnson later in this narrative. All three of these brothers were born in Edgefield District South Carolina. So, in a way to speculate and appease the doubt that existed in Zachariah's place of birth, it was concluded that our Zachariah was possibly born in Edgefield District as well.

Records are available to confirm the father of these three boys of our ancestral heritage and their place of birth. The only problem is making a factual and conclusive connection to the correct Zachariah. As we try to make the connections of the spouse and/or the parents of Zachariah, or when and how he came to this area, we are at a loss and are now left to assumptions and the possible connection of records and we are then left to guessing or deductive reasoning. This led to the finding and tracing of several Johnson records in England, Ireland and Scotland during this period as we have mentioned.

Another Zachariah Johnson can be traced to England around 1740 with his records of christening in Elsham, Lincoln, England on August 19, 1739. His father was William Johnson and his mother was Elizabeth Johnson. This Zachariah Johnson did land in Charleston, South Carolina. Perhaps this is the same Zachariah Johnson that we are trying to connect to our ancestral history.

As we explored the many records we were finally led to these records found in Elsham, Lincoln, England in the early 1700s. Of all the records searched we finally discovered birth records of this child named Zachariah and his Christening in 1739.

We knew that our Zachariah would have been born around 1738-1740. Of all the records explored, there was only one family record that has a son named Zachariah in the Scotland, Ireland or England area, with parents named William and Elizabeth and with a son named Zachariah that will closely connect the dots. Since we know that Zachariah named one of his sons (his first) William, then we have a suspicion that this was a family name and was probably passed down through the generations. The name Elizabeth has also appeared on numerous occasions in our genealogy. We will also discover that this was common for the Johnsons in another name that will become important in our line of the Johnson clan and was passed down. We will make this name known later.

Keep in mind that there are also many William Johnsons in England but as we search these, we can only find one set of records of a William Johnson and his spouse Elizabeth with a son named Zachariah. William and Elizabeth had a son born and christened him on August 19, 1739 in Elsham, Lincolnshire, England. The birth date fits with the facts that are already known.

Although we have always known of Zachariah in our history of distant relatives, we have never known his wife's name. In Union

County South Carolina, there is a Probate Will that was recorded of a Zachariah Johnson declaring that he is leaving his farm of 120 acres, all his livestock, his household items and all property to his wife named Sara Johnson. This "will" also states that he has three other family members that the property will go to at his wife, Sara's death. These would be his sons. This places this Zachariah Johnson in the same area of South Carolina as the three mentioned Johnson boys listed birthplaces.

Nothing is certain of our Johnson Clan until we arrive in Edgefield District South Carolina in 1740. It is known that this Zachariah Johnson did indeed first land in Charleston S.C. It has always been believed that our Johnsons first arrived in America at Charleston, South Carolina. There was an enclave of Scottish-Irish in the Carolinas, which was drawing, more and more of the Scots and Irish to the Carolinas each year. This is believed to be the first entry in to the New America for this Johnson Clan. With this information and records we are led to believe that this is the same Zachariah Johnson who had a son named Jeremiah of whom we are descendants.

Edgefield district was designated as a district prior to its extensive settlement, when the American colonists began to slowly move southward and inland. This district is west of Charleston and on the western side of South Carolina. Cattlemen or drovers, had discovered the richness of the South Carolina area as they brought their herds southward to graze on the rich grasslands. When they were fattened, they would take their cattle back to the populated areas for sale. One of these cattle drovers was John Stevens who in 1715 began to fatten his cattle in this area. Stevens Creek, S.C. was named after him. As the cattlemen brought back exciting and positive information of the area, more and more colonists began to migrate to South Carolina.

In the late sixteen nineties, Scotland and northern England were having a terrible famine. There was never an exact number placed on the lives lost during this terrible time of inclement weather and failed crops, but the death toll from starvation and malnutrition was in the thousands.

During this same period a trading company was formed to trade in Africa and the Indies. England quickly blocked them from establishing trade in any part of the world. Thus, a businessman named William Patterson decided to form his own company, Darien Trading Company, and go it alone. The owner found the ideal time to encourage Scottish investors to join the company. Not only were the Scots going through a difficult time with the famine but the Scots objection to England trying to control their every move was highly resented. The efforts and well publicized blocking of any international trade by the trading company only tended to infuriate the Scots even more.

People began to invest their last savings in Patterson's plan. There was a strip of land in Panama that he had named the Darien Isthmus. His plan was to take the investors and begin a colony on this strip of land. The people were anxious to leave Scotland, their political problems and the struggle for survival behind them. The people were told that this land was the "Key to the Universe". From this area in Panama they could control all the trade of the world and the people were gullible in accepting this as fact and were swept along in the fervor for this new adventure. They, along with Patterson would become wealthy as they capitalized on the multitude of trade coming through this area and bound for America and Scotland or England. The company raised hundreds of thousands of pounds for their venture.

What the people did not know was that this isthmus of land was nothing more than a fly infested and fever blighted swamp of Panama that was already claimed by the country of Spain. For the next two years, the small colony struggled against odds in which they could not win. There were the constant problems with Spain concerning the claims to the lands. There were problems with the native people of Panama and the constant torrential rain that made their lives a living hell. Their clothes and shoes rotted, their food stocks and goods became infested with weevils, mildewed and rotted. They suffered from constant disease and they died by the dozens. Patterson's wife died from disease and Patterson himself almost died. Finally, after being abandoned by William, King of England who refused to help, Spain came to the rescue and took aboard a ship, the remaining 300 colonists who had survived out of the 1,200 original occupants. They all returned to Scotland totally ruined from their investment and their adventure.

—————

CHAPTER 10

THERE WERE AT LEAST 29 different tribes of Indians in the South Carolina area. The survival of the early colonists greatly depended on the relations between the Indians and the early settlers. For the most part the Indian tribes were friendly and they assisted the settlers in this area although it would cost them greatly as the increasing population of white settlers slowly swallowed up and claimed their land. Diseases that were never known to exist in the Indian populations, were introduced by the settlers. These diseases claimed the lives of literally thousands of Native Indians. The Johnsons would as residents of South Carolina realize firsthand the conflicts that were brewing.

In 1753, the French and British were having territorial claims disputes concerning land in the Ohio Valley area. The French and Indian War was over these same issues. These disputes led to skirmishes along the borders and led to the French building several forts along a line from Lake Erie to the Ohio River near present day Pittsburgh. The British considered this a hostile act and ordered the French to disassemble the forts and thereby began to reinforce its troops in this area as well. In 1754, the French and British were both trying to gain favor of the Indians to support their side of the disagreements. The Iroquois Confederation of Indians and the British advanced a plan to bring this group of Indians, namely the Mingoes, to their side by giving one of the

Native Americans, Tanaghrisson, the title of "Half King" over the Mingoes and other Native American groups under the Iroquois rule. The Indians had their problems with both the French and the British but felt that the greater danger for them was with the British, who they felt (rightfully so) were trying to take over the Indian Territory. They considered the lesser of the two evils to be with the French and therefore aligned with the French.

The British- French war, better known as the "Seven Year War" began because of these territorial disputes and lasted until 1763. The war ended with the "Treaty of Paris" in 1763. France had lost this war and would hold a bitter grudge against the British, which would again re-surface in 1775.

With the outbreak of these wars in the Ohio Valley area many of the settlers in the area began to relocate further south, with many ending up in Virginia and North Carolina. Some even ventured further south to the rich lands that they had heard of in South Carolina. One area in the western side of South Carolina was known as the "Edgefield District" and Zachariah Johnson's family ended up in this district to raise their family. Zachariah's wife was unknown except from the recorded will of one Zachariah Johnson and she was named Sara but there are records of their three sons Shadrach, William and Jeremiah and their marriage into the mixed Indian population.

This area of South Carolina was known for its rich and fertile soil and the land was available for grants. This was the appeal to many of the early settlers. The larger the family, the larger the land grants. This was an incentive for the farmers coming to this area. Many of the land grants were for 120 acres.

Historical records indicate that as young men, these three sons of Zachariah were intent on supporting the American Colonists political views against the ever-increasing pressure placed on the colonists by the British rulers. These differences finally came to a head in 1775, when war broke out. However, this time it was the British and the Americans in the Revolutionary War or "The American War for Independence".

All three of Zachariah's sons, William born in 1756, Shadrach, born in 1759 and then Jeremiah who was born in 1761 are found in records and all were involved in the Revolutionary War. There is no evidence that the father Zachariah was involved in the war. His age and family may have been a factor, although he would only have been thirty-six years of age at the outbreak of the American Revolution and his youngest son, Jeremiah, would have been a young sixteen years of age. Records indicate that at least one, and probably all three young men served as Revolutionary soldiers in the Newbury District, of Charleston, and of South Carolina.

Shadrach Johnson was born in 1759 and moved from the Edgefield District to an area known as Fairfield, S.C. He was married and became the father of ten children but most records of these children are lost. However, one set of records indicates that one of Shadrach's sons, named William, was born in S.C. in 1775 and married a lady named Johanna. Her last name is unknown. This William and his family later moved to Choctaw County, Mississippi and records show that they lived there in 1850 as recorded in the 1850 census. This also coincides with other descendants from Shadrach's brother Jeremiah, who would eventually reside in this area of Mississippi along with an Indian population.

After the Revolutionary War the sons of Zachariah Johnson began to marry and drift to other areas. Jeremiah Johnson, first went to North Carolina where he met a beautiful lady who had satin black hair, a beautiful dark completion and bright blue eyes, which reminded one of the mixed blood of the European settlers and the native Indians. This lady's name was Comfort Brown. Her parents had settled in North Carolina. Her father was John H. Brown born in 1740 and her mother was Martha Ann Kell, born in 1742. Jeremiah and Comfort were married in North Carolina but they quickly made their way back to the Edgefield, S.C. area where they started their large family. Jeremiah remained in Edgefield District, now Edgefield County after the Revolutionary War, as did his brother Shadrach. Shadrach can now be traced to Union County, South Carolina where it is stated that he married and had several children. His wife's name is unknown lending to speculation that he had married an Indian woman or mixed Indian as well, since that area of South Carolina had a heavy population of Indians. The years of birth of Shadrach's ten children are known and are listed as six girls born in 1793, 1795, 1796, 1800, 1802 and 1810. Also listed are four sons whose years of birth are listed as 1797, 1799, 1805, and 1807.

From this point, we cannot follow Shadrach beyond South Carolina, except for a Revolutionary War document that was discovered. This document is from a filing in court in which Shadrach Johnson is presenting evidence to the court which declares that he served in the Revolutionary War and declares his birth date. The purpose of the filing was for a war pension. His date of filing is listed as 1832 and states that he is a revolutionary war veteran. This document states with witnesses, that he has always lived in and around the Chesterfield District of South Carolina. It gives his age as seventy-one but also states that his father, who would be a verifiable witness to his claims, is dead. His father would be Zachariah Johnson. This would be the same age of our Shadrach Johnson.

CHAPTER 11

———

THE NEWLY DECLARED CONTINENTAL CONGRESS announced its independence in 1776 and then formerly declared its independence on
July 4, 1776. Yet this war for independence would continue until
1783. France's anger with the British would now resurface as the
French supported the Revolutionists with weapons and artillery.
Their navy played a great part in shutting off the British route of
escape in Yorktown. Spain would also join in the efforts by supporting the revolutionists with weapons and ammunition.

Count Rochambeau of France, joined with the revolutionists
and is given credit as a brilliant strategist and being the main
force that pushed the 8,000 remaining British forces back to
Yorktown. Overnight the American forces moved a short distance from the British forces and quietly dug a long trench
which placed them nearer the British forces. When morning
came, they began their attack upon the surprised British and
quickly had them on the run. The problem was that the British
had very little distance from them and the bay. They expected
the British fleet to come to their rescue. Now they were in for
another surprise. The French fleet had come to the aid of the
American Revolutionists. They had sailed into the bay and cut
off the British fleet. The newly arrived French fleet prevented
the British escape and kept the British fleet at a distance. All
those British forces were captured or killed. The battleground

area near Yorktown is a national park area with all its history of the battles that took place there. The Americans had gained their independence with the British defeat. The British then recognized the American independence from the British yoke and the territorial boundaries were set as bounded by Canada to the north, the Mississippi river to the west and Florida to the south.

Although the war with the American colonists had ended, Britain continued their war with France and Spain who were now heavily involved in Florida and claimed Florida as their territory. That war ended in 1783, with another "Treaty of Paris". Yes, the French had their revenge over the British but gained little more, as one writer reported, no more "than a huge national debt".

The Spanish however maintained that its boundaries were different than those accepted by the British and the Americans. Because of this difference concerning where the boundaries were, the Spanish closed off all navigation rights to the Americans and the main port at New Orleans was closed to all goods being shipped to or from the American states. In 1795, the border disagreement was settled, and the U.S. and Spain again had a trade agreement. New Orleans was reopened, and Americans could again transfer goods without paying cargo fees (right of deposit) when they transferred goods from one ship to another. This dispute would be resolved with the "Treaty of San Lorenzo" or also known as "Pinckney's Treaty" in 1795 and also included that the Americans would have navigation rights of the Mississippi River. As stated by Gerald H. Clairfield, this treaty simply stated that it "Established Friendly Intentions" between the two nations.

After the American Revolutionary War, Spain claimed the British border on the day the Treaty of Paris was signed, but the United States insisted on the old boundary. This boundary had been in dispute since the kingdom of Great Britain had expanded the territory of the Florida colonies while it was in its possession.

It had moved the boundary from the 31st parallel northwards to a line drawn due east from the junction of the Yazoo River and the Mississippi River, which is the present-day location of Vicksburg, Mississippi

In 1803, the U.S. purchased land from the French. This purchase became known as the "Louisiana Purchase" in which a vast amount of territory was purchased from the French for $15,000,000. France now had relinquished all claims of land south of the now Canadian and U.S. border. The land purchased was only the territory that was claimed by the French but this land actually belonged to the Indian tribes who had inhabited this vast area before there were any French present on the North American continent.

The Native Indians were again caught up in these territorial disputes, which included lands that they alone had claimed for generations. All negotiations were between governments which had little or no consideration of the American Indians. They were always treated as unimportant. Now the Indians were forced to accept the boundary lines agreed upon in the "Treaty of Lorenz" as being north of the present Georgia and Florida lines. Although many of the Indians were now forced to move from Florida and above these accepted lines, there were many who refused to be displaced from the lands that were theirs. They would not accept the agreement between the U.S and other countries.

Following the war of 1812 the west played an ever-increasing role in the American settlers western movement. There became a power struggle of this western movement as it began to involve the politicians, such as congressmen and senators. They began to support the various citizen delegations that were intent on taking over the Indian lands. The Florida Indians were forced to migrate first to Alabama, then to Mississippi then further to the west.

In 1819, the Cherokee, Creek, Choctaw, Chickasaw, Creek and Seminole Indians were pressured by the America government to sell their lands for mere pennies per acre. The "Adams Onis

Treaty" of 1819, also known as the "Transcontinental Treaty" was signed into law. The favorite title for this Treaty in American history books is the "Florida Purchase". Florida had become a burden to Spain. They could no longer afford to maintain its garrisons of soldiers in Florida. Spain decided to divest itself of all its claims by negotiating a sale to the U.S. This treaty was the culmination of the sale of the Spanish claimed Florida territory. The United States purchased the territory for $5,000,000. Now the new boundaries were set at the Sabine River through the Rocky Mountains to the west coast. This line would run from the Sabine River in Louisiana, north of present day New Mexico, Utah, Arizona and California. This territory south of the transcontinental line and the territory mentioned above would become yet another land area that would be contested in future years and with a government that had been virtually excluded in past negotiations. The land of Texas and the now state of Texas had seen its disagreements and wars with its southern neighbor of Mexico. General Santa Anna was leading the Mexican army.

Santa Anna was the Mexican General who attacked the Texans at the Alamo in 1836, killing 189 Texas defenders and at Goliad, where he ordered the execution of four hundred Texas prisoners. This led to an all-out war with Mexico by the then territory of Texas. Santa Anna was soundly defeated by the Texans at San Jacinto in east Texas and was captured while trying to escape dressed in a dragoon privates uniform. History records that Santa Anna spent days crying and pleading for his life. He was later given his freedom and allowed to return to his Hacienda in Vera Cruise. Santa Anna was later exiled to Cuba by Mexican authorities. In 1836 Texas, had won its independence from Mexico in the Texas Revolution.

Santa Anna, while in exile, convinced President Polk that if the he was supported by the U.S. in his return to Mexico he would end the dispute in favor of the U.S. However, when he returned he quickly took control of the Mexican army and led the Mexican troops into battle. He was defeated at Buena Vista with heavy losses to his troops. He returned to Mexico City and took over the presidency of Mexico. Although defeated at Vera Cruz and the battle of Buena Vista he was still determined to end the dispute over the territory near the Rio Grande but it would be in favor of Mexico.

Mexico and the U.S would both contest the others claims to the territory, which would now be resolved with the Mexican American War of 1848. Santa Anna still held a grudge against Texas after his defeat in the revolution. The Texans had decided their own destiny and rebelled against the Mexican government's claims that they controlled Texas, which began the dispute.

Then in 1846 Texas which was now a part of the United States, began to experience intrusions from Mexico and its military. There had remained a disputed zone between the Rio Grande River and the Neches River in Texas. Mexico claimed that this was their territory and the U.S. made the same claim. The Mexican Army attacked U.S. soldiers in Coahuila killing twelve and taking fifty-two prisoners. War broke out between the U.S. and Mexico because of this intrusion into the disputed territory. This resulted in the first war that the United States would fight on foreign soil.

President James Polk was a staunch believer in "Manifest Destiny" and was therefore adamant on the U.S. expansion to the Pacific Ocean to the west. In 1847 General Winfield Scott landed in Veracruz (previously known as Vera Cruz) and quickly occupied the city. In the ensuing war, the United States Army, led by General Zachary Taylor, drove the Mexican army back to Mexico City and beyond. The result of the Mexican defeat in the Mexican-American War was the "Treaty of Guadalupe Hidalgo" in 1848. Santa Anna and the Mexican Government agreed, as stated in the treaty, that Mexico would give up certain specified lands to the United States, including the disputed land in Texas. That land now makes up the states of California, Utah and Nevada, as well as parts of Colorado, Wyoming, New Mexico and

Arizona. The treaty also established the undisputed national border of Mexico at the Rio Grande River. Even today, many Mexicans state incorrectly, that the United States stole this land from Mexico. History records that it was purchased from Mexico for fifteen million dollars as part of the settlement of the Mexican-American War in which Mexico was soundly defeated by the U.S. This was a war that had been instigated by Mexico but resulted in a now defined border.

———◆———

CHAPTER 12

THE INDIANS WERE NOW BEGINNING a phase in their history that would take them from their native lands and force them to migrate from one area to other areas in the future. They would suffer hardship after hardship resulting in thousands of deaths, as they were forced to abandon one settled area after another and being forced to finally move to the Oklahoma territory.

In the south, there remained about 60,000 Choctaw, Cherokee, Chickasaw, Creek and Seminole Indians. In 1819, monies were appropriated by the legislature to train the Indians in ways of agriculture and Christianity. The plan worked as many of the Native Americans eagerly accepted the white man's way of life - so much so that the whites began to call these tribes "The Five Civilized Tribes". Even as these methods were instrumented, the white settlers began to encroach and settle on the Native American lands that had not been ceded to the Government. The final results were that president James Monroe recommended that the Indian tribes be removed from their lands to a specific area west of the Mississippi River.

In 1820, the Treaty of "Doaks Stand" was signed in which the Choctaw Nation was convinced to give up virtually half of the Choctaw Nations land in Tennessee, Alabama northern Mississippi, Arkansas and Louisiana for land west of the Mississippi River and known as Oklahoma Territory. They maintained part of the land in what is now known as Neshoba County, Mississippi. Neshoba will at a future date become a sad part of the Johnson history in this narrative.

The Indians would always proclaim that Andrew Jackson, who would later become president, had tricked them into accepting inferior lands for their tribal lands. Jackson had finally resorted to threats in order to pressure and/or persuade the Indians to sign the treaty, telling them "Many of your nation are already beyond the Mississippi, and others are being removed every year-----if you refuse your nation (*your, meaning the Cherokee Nation*) will be destroyed." The treaty was signed by the chiefs on October 18, 1820. They would always insist that they were forced to sign the treaty because of the threats from Andrew Jackson.

Jeremiah Johnson, his wife Comfort Brown and their children moved in 1795, to Fairfield County, S.C. to be near his older brother Shadrach. Jeremiah and Comfort had a total of seven children. They began their family in South Carolina.

The oldest brother, William Johnson born in Edgefield District in 1756, moved first to Georgia and later moved to Loundes, Dallas County, Alabama. His death is listed as April 23,1854. Here we have another of the Johnson clan who lived 98 years. He is also listed in the 1850, U.S. Census in Dallas County, Alabama.

Jeremiah eventually traveled to Alabama by way of Georgia where his brother William had moved and lived for a short period of time before both families eventually moved to Dallas County, Alabama

The U.S. Census of 1822, lists Jeremiah, his wife Comfort and their children in Dallas County, Alabama. Also, listed in the census are William Johnson and his family. This placed the Johnson family in the very Indian Territory that was undergoing such upheaval and turmoil. They were attracted to these surroundings because of Comfort Brown's Indian heritage and their children showed this Indian heritage as well. While in Dallas County, another child was born to Jeremiah and Comfort Brown that was listed in the census only as child, perhaps meaning that the child had died at birth. No other records are shown for this child.

Jeremiah, Comfort Brown and their children would later follow their son Zattie Johnson to Mississippi, where they were again associated with the Indian tribes of Neshoba County. Jeremiah and Comfort's children are mentioned here because we will follow some of these children and the interesting history that is attached to them.

The "****" indicates the Johnson family member that will be followed in this narrative which connects with our lineage of the Johnsons.

Thomas A. Johnson was born in 1798 in Edgefield District S.C. and died in 1865 near Birmingham, Alabama
****Zattie Johnson** was born in 1802 in Edgefield District was married in Dallas County, Alabama to Margaret Anna Evans on December 13, 1826.

Zattie is mentioned here also because in 1911, another Johnson from this lineage of Johnsons was born in Bradley County, Arkansas and would be named Zattie after his uncle who lived one hundred years earlier. There is also another Zattie descendant who lived in Winn Parish, Louisiana who will be a part of the Johnson history at a later date.

William Johnson (Jeremiah's son) was born in Edgefield District in 1804 and he and his wife both died in 1877 in Neshoba County, Mississippi.
George Washington Johnson was born in Edgefield District in 1812
John F. Johnson was born in Edgefield District in 1814 and died in Bradley County, Arkansas in 1876.

Francis Johnson was born in 1818 in Dallas County, Alabama.

Shadrach Hubert Johnson was born in Autauga County, Alabama on March 6, 1833.

As we follow the life of Jeremiah Johnson and his family's short stay with his brother Shadrach (the first Shadrach born in 1759) near Fairfield South Carolina, the trek turns to the states farther south. By 1822, the census shows that the Jeremiah Johnson family was living in Dallas County Alabama and confirms that he is married to Comfort Brown, an Indian woman believed to be of Cherokee descent. This area is west of Montgomery, Alabama and has as its county seat, Selma, Alabama. Dallas County is a county with rich soil that encouraged the influx of settlers from the first mention of its prospects of great crop production for the farmers. Dallas County would also prove to be rich in its history of slavery throughout the early to mid-1860s, and its involvement in the civil war. It would also find its way into history in the 1960s, as the civil rights movement was underway. One of Martin Luther King's civil rights marches took place in Selma, Alabama which is in Dallas County and is the County Seat.

Several years later in the history of the Johnson Family, one of the Johnsons would return to this area, start a family and then return to the Arkansas area.

Jeremiah's son, Zattie Johnson was the first born and his birth is listed as being in Edgefield County S.C. in 1802. In 1826, Jeremiah's son Zattie Johnson married Margaret Ann Williams of Dallas County, Alabama. Zattie's son, who he named Shadrach, after his brother, was born in Autauga County, Alabama in 1833.

CHAPTER 13

In 1830, the "Treaty of Dancing Rabbit" was signed and was officially proclaimed in 1831. This treaty was signed by the Choctaw Indians and the U.S. Government and became the first of the Indian removal treaties under the Removal Act. This act ceded about 11 million acres of the Choctaw Nation in the state of Mississippi, Tennessee, and south western Kentucky to the United States Government for about 15 million acres in Oklahoma territory which was bounded be the Red River to the south, and to the present Arkansas border near Ft. Smith to the east. The Choctaw nation was allowed to retain some of their land in Mississippi and these Indians became the first non-European people to gain citizenship in the U.S.

The Choctaw Nation now became two nations, The Choctaw nation of Oklahoma and the Choctaw Tribe of Neshoba, Mississippi.

In 1832, the Chickasaw Nation signed a treaty with the U.S. government. This was "The Treaty of Pontotoc Creek". This treaty gave up all the lands owned by the Chickasaws, east of the Mississippi for lands west of the Mississippi. The Chickasaw would be allowed to have their own government in the new territory because they stated, "They could not live by the laws and rules of the white man". Their lands were in Tennessee, Mississippi and Alabama. Their new land would also be in Oklahoma territory. Their lands would adjoin the Choctaw Indian lands. These two tribes had problems between them in the past. Now they would be forced to reconcile their differences and live as neighbors throughout history.

In this treaty, the U.S. Government agreed to transfer all monies received from the sale of the land, less expenses, to the Chickasaw Nation. Minimum price was settled on at $3.00 per acre and that price would later be bargained down. In total, the land was surveyed out at 6,283,804 acres of which certain numbers of acres would be set aside to be allotted for schools and mail routes through the land, as stated in the treaties. However, the total amount was later determined by the U.S. Government to be 174,000 acres that were needed for the allotted schools and routes. This was land that the Indians were not paid for.

The resulting movement of the Native Indian Tribes has been termed as the "Trail of Tears". The Trail of Tears was so named because of the terrible hardship, illness and disease suffered by the Indians on their forced movement west. We will look at the route in which the Indians were taken to the destination of their newly assigned lands in Oklahoma and southern Kansas. This trail led to Tennessee, southern Kentucky, Missouri, Arkansas and then to Oklahoma. One route of the several that were eventually used brought the Indians northward through Tennessee to Southern Illinois then back down the flow of the Mississippi River to Arkansas then followed the Arkansas river toward Oklahoma. The Choctaw Indians would be the first Native Americans to travel the Trail of Tears. However, the Cherokee would suffer the most during this disastrous removal. They suffered from exposure to the harsh winter, disease, and starvation. There were various routes taken during the removal process. Some of these routes were later seen as totally unreasonable.

In 1838, the U.S. army began their enforcement of the Removal Act. They began rounding up the Cherokee Indians and held them in stockades. Over 3,000 Cherokees were placed on boats to travel to the new territory. The travel took them to the Tennessee,

Ohio and Mississippi rivers, then to Arkansas and into the Indian Territory. There were over 14,000 Cherokee who remained in prison camps until the winter of 1838-1839. They were then marched through Tennessee, Kentucky, Illinois, Missouri and Arkansas. During this march through torrential rains, inclement weather conditions and a shortage of food, water and proper clothing, over 4,000 Indians perished.

Many Indians were moved originally from the Florida, Alabama, and Mississippi tribal lands and even west of the Mississippi River into Louisiana. Even today there are still small contingents of the Choctaw and Cherokee Indians in Alabama, Texas and Louisiana. Other tribes were moved west through Louisiana, Arkansas and Texas. There remained in Florida a large contingent of Seminole Indians who refused to leave their native lands.

Zattie Johnson, son of Jeremiah Johnson and his wife remained in Autauga County, Alabama where two of their children were born. They finally moved to Neshoba County, Mississippi in 1836 and another child Deborah L. Johnson was born to him and his wife in 1838. Although the family was in an Indian community they still did not feel safe. The settlers were creating problems for the Indians but antagonism was also displayed toward the mixed Indian people.

The Johnsons felt it was no longer safe for the Indian-American mixed family to remain in Alabama. Jeremiah, Zattie and William moved and relocated to the Indian lands in Neshoba County, Mississippi, as many of the Choctaw Indians (the dividing of the Choctaw nations into two) had begun to relocate to their new homeland in the Oklahoma territory. The Johnsons would remain for a few years, in the same area of the Indians who were staying in the now smaller Choctaw lands of Neshoba County

In 1838, land opportunities were being made available in Arkansas. Jeremiah and his son, Zattie and their families now relocated to Union County, Arkansas. Other Families were also relocating to this new area. Some of the families leaving the Neshoba, Mississippi area were the Branches, Carters, Hairston, Williams, Hargis, Thompson, Ferguson, Hodges, Hamiltons and Simmons. Several of these families will become related to the Johnsons through marriage. Some of these settlers would later play a prominent role in their areas of settlement.

Although his father and brothers left for Arkansas, William, son of Jeremiah and his family decided to remain in Neshoba County, Mississippi. Williams's descendants would remain there for the next one hundred fifty years. Nearly one hundred thirty years later one of the descendants of William would be involved in a crime that would become known throughout the world. We will include in this narrative, the story of this horrible and humiliating incident at a later time in our narrative.

From their first entry into America at Charleston, South Carolina, the Johnsons had always been southerners. It wasn't until after World War II, that some of the Johnson clan began to migrate to the north.

———

CHAPTER 14

As we now follow Jeremiah and his children, we will specifically follow Zattie and Margaret Ann's family. Margaret Ann was born in Dallas County, Alabama where she and Zattie were married and started their family.

Their children are listed as follows.

**** **John Evan Johnson** was born in Dallas County, Alabama in 1830. It was stated that he was blessed with a dark, smooth, golden skin and complexion and with hazel eyes and coal black hair. Here we have an indication of his mixed Indian heritage. This description of John Evan was later found in his civil war enlistment papers.

Soon after John Evan was born, Zattie Johnson and his family moved across the county line to Autauga County, Alabama so he could begin work with Shadrach Williams who owned a cotton spinning and weaving mill. He also owned a corn grinding grist mill and Zattie would become employed as Shadrach Williams' slave foreman.

While under this employment, another son was born to Zattie and his wife and they named him after his employer, Shadrach, or perhaps after his uncle, Shadrach Johnson. **Shadrach Hubert Johnson** was born in March 6, 1833. He also had a dark complexion with black hair and hazel eyes as did his brother John Evan.

The American Indian heritage was showing up in the complexion of these children.

Two other children were born in Autauga County. These children were;

Susan M. Johnson, 1834 and
Thomas F. Johnson, born in 1835.

When the Johnsons heard of the Indian Treaties that we have mentioned, they were unsure if they would be allowed to move directly to their desired location of Arkansas. They first moved to Neshoba County, Mississippi. While in Neshoba County, another child, a daughter, was born. **Deborah L. Johnson** was born in 1838.

Jeremiah's family began to disperse to several areas. Zattie moved to the area of Winn Parish in central Louisiana sometime just prior to the 1850, U.S. Census where Jeremiah would later join him. Jeremiah would then be in his late eighties. His wife died in 1843 and was buried in Huttig, Union County, Arkansas. The census of 1850, lists Jeremiah as being 89 years old. Here we have a difference of places of death. Not in recorded death certificates but in the family genealogy. Some had recorded erroneous information concerning burial plots in the cemetery at Union County, Arkansas. One record of genealogy incorrectly states that Jeremiah's Indian wife died in 1843, and is buried in Huttig Cemetery in Union County, Arkansas and that "her husband is also buried there". However, other records including census reports and future death certificates record the factual information. The Census records indicate that Jeremiah had left Union County, Arkansas and relocated to Winn Parish, Louisiana to be with his son Zattie.

Jeremiah's son Zattie Johnson decided to relocate to Winn Parish, Louisiana after his mother Comfort Brown Johnson, died in 1843. This would have made his move prior to the census of

1850. He would spend the rest of his life in Winn Parish. Why he decided to leave the Arkansas area is not known nor is the reason he chose to go to Winn Parish, Louisiana known. The census of 1850, lists Zattie Johnson and his family along with his father, Jeremiah Johnson as being in Winn Parish, Louisiana. This document also lists Zattie and his wife Margaret Ann's children.

Death records of Winn Parish and cemetery burial records list Jeremiah's death as 1860, in Winn, Parish at the age of 99. These are documented records and are the factual records as recorded in the U.S. census and death records. However, one error does exist in the death certificate. That is his age. We know that Jeremiah was born in Edgefield District, South Carolina in 1761. With this information and the actual date and year of his death in Winn Parish, we can conclude that Jeremiah had, as had several of his relatives from the Johnson Clan, lived a long life of 99 years. Yet we discovered in the hand written, death certificate placed in the records of Winn Parish, someone listed his birth date incorrectly and published that he had died "Of Old Age" at the age of 106 years. We have had, in the Johnson Clan; several relatives live to be in their late nineties. Jeremiah has produced some good genes, but the actual age at his death was ninety-nine.

The end of this chapter includes an actual copy of the U.S. Census from 1850, in Winn Parish, Louisiana of Zattie Johnson and his household. Notice the last names listed of the household members. It shows that Jeremiah had indeed gone to Winn Parish after the death of his wife, Comfort Brown, in 1843. At the time of the census in 1850 in Winn Parish, his age is shown to be eighty-nine. He was in Bradley County, Arkansas when his wife died, so he apparently left after her death, for Winn Parrish where he lived until his death in 1860, as shown in Winn Parish death records.

Zattie, Jeremiah Johnson's older son then lived until his death in 1878, in Winn Parish and his wife lived with their son Shadrach and his wife until her death one year later in 1879. They are both buried in Shady Grove Cemetery between Winnfield, Louisiana and Olla, Louisiana.

Now we will address another issue found in the U.S. Census report of 1850. It is unclear who the two men are and why they were living with the Johnson family. Although their names are listed as John Nobles and William Fike, the men are a mystery as to their relationship to the family. An earlier U.S. Census lists two black servants living with their household when they were in Alabama. This was the time or shortly after the period when Zattie was working for a plantation owner and grist mill owner who was also a slave owner. Perhaps these are the two men listed here and had moved with the Zattie and Jeremiah Johnson families as they relocated. However, this census of 1850, listed their race as white. This is a copy of a typed report compiled years later and the hand-written form filled out by the Zattie Johnson household, which clearly shows two white men. If these two men were indeed associated with the two black servants, or were indeed the black servants, why would Zattie Johnson fill out the form and list these two men as white? Or was an error made in the typed report? If this was indeed the two black servants living with the Zattie Johnson household instead of two white men as they listed them in the census, it makes one wonder why he did not disclose this in the census. If it was an error made in the transferring of the information to a typed report then the error would not have been intentional.

In an earlier Alabama census report of 1830, from Alabama, Jeremiah Johnson lists two black females in his household who were servants. This time also correlates with the same time period when Zattie was working as a slave foreman. One is a girl between eight to ten years of age and another is a female who was listed as being between 20-25 years of age. The older is probably the mother of the younger. Now! Were the two female servants somehow exchanged, as was often the case with masters of the black slaves, for the two men? We will never know the facts or truth of the mystery.

If the above mentioned is indeed correct, then it would not be a proud time for the Johnson family. This census also shows that in the Census of 1850, the two men were born in Alabama but does not give any additional information. This could then be traced back to the time when in the 1830s, the Jeremiah and Zattie Johnson families were in Alabama and did indeed have black servants in their household. Were these two men actually servants who had remained loyal to the Jeremiah Johnson family for over thirty years? We do not know the answer.

Zattie Johnson	1802	Male	48	White	1802	Male	48
John Evin Johnson	1850	Male	22	White	1828	Alabama	589
Shadrach Johnson	1853	Male	20	White	1830	Alabama	589
Susanna M Johnson	1850	Female	17	White	1833	Alabama	589
Thos H Johnson	1850	Male	15	White	1835	Alabama	589
Debra L Johnson	1850	Female	12	White	1838	Mississippi	589
Julia A Johnson	1850	Female	7	White	1843	Arkansas	589
Frances E Johnson	1850	Female	4	White	1846	Arkansas	589
Coleman G Johnson	1850	Male	2	White	1848	Arkansas	589
Wm Fike	1850	Male	35	White	1815	Alabama	594
Jno Nobles	1850	Male	25	White	1825	Alabama	594
Jeremiah Johnson	1850	Male	89	White	1761	South Carolina	590

—————

SOUTH CAROLINA WAS AN AREA of major importance during the American Civil War, both politically and militarily. The rich and fertile land in South Carolina continued to draw farmers to the region. Tobacco and Cotton were the major crops but these highly sought after products were also labor intensive. As the need for labor increased with the growing farms and plantations, the slave labor began to increase. By 1860, the white population in South Carolina was 291,300. Yet as we look at the slave population it was substantially larger than the white population. Even in 1790, the slave population and the white population were almost equal with white population at 140,000 and the black population at 108,000. Yet by 1860, the white population had grown to 291,000 while the black population had exploded to over 412,000.

In 1860, one report stated that South Carolina, had the highest percentage of slaves of any U.S. state. With 57% of its population enslaved and 46% of its families owning at least one slave.

1790		1820	
White	Black	White	Black
140,178	108,895	237,440	265,301
1840		1860	
White	Black	White	Black
259,084	335,314	291,300	412,320

Although the Scottish people would like to deny that they had ever been a part of the slave trade, it just is not the case. We need only to look at the many names that were adopted by the slaves and we quickly detect that many of those names are of Scottish origin. Most slaves adopted the names of their owners. We have the names of Campbell, Douglas, Graham, MacDonald, MacFarlane, Morrison, Robinson, Stewart and many others.

There were some recorded Scottish ships that were involved in transporting slaves to America and returning with a cargo of tobacco for the Scottish tobacco lords.

South Carolina became the first state to secede from the U.S. and the first Civil War battle was fought there, with the first shots being fired at Ft. Sumter. On April 12, 1861, forces under the command of General Beauregard began bombarding the fort. These were the first shots of the war, and continued all day, watched by many civilians in a spirit of celebration. The fort had been cut off from its supply line and surrendered the next day.

The Second Battle of Fort Sumter (September 8, 1863) was a failed attempt by the Union to re-take the fort. The attempt failed in part due to rivalry between army and navy commanders. Although the fort was reduced to rubble, it remained in Confederate hands until it was evacuated as Sherman marched through South Carolina in February 1865.

South Carolina became a major source for troops for the confederacy during the war. It is also a fact in history that the Union Army benefited from men from South Carolina. Thousands of freed slaves flocked to join the Union Forces. The state also provided uniforms, textiles, food, and war material, as well as trained soldiers and leaders from the Citadel Military College and other military schools. The Citadel continues today to produce some of Americas finest military men and women.

While living in Winn Parish, Louisiana, Zattie Johnson's oldest son, John Evan Johnson, met and married Mary Catherine Williams. She was born in Alabama on February 6, 1839. Her parents were originally from Georgia and had relocated, as had the Johnsons, to Alabama.

A son was born to the young couple on May 23, 1859, and they named him ******William Jasper Johnson**. We will follow William Jasper Johnson and his life a little later in this writing as one of the Johnson family's embarrassing and dark moments in history occurred.

Just as the Civil war began in South Carolina, South Carolina was the first to quickly secede from the U.S. This secession was then rapidly followed by ten other states with five border states joining. One of those states was Louisiana. There was a great need for men and there was a great need for Confederate dollars throughout the south.

John Evan Johnson was one of those young men with a young family in desperate need of those Confederate dollars. At twenty-four years of age, John Evan Johnson went to Monroe, Louisiana and joined the Confederate States of America army on June 7th, 1862. He joined Company I of the 29th Louisiana Division. As a payment for him joining, John Evan received a payment of $50.00.

The Confederate enlistment records show that John Evan was a slim 160 pounder with a florid complexion (red or ruby or rosy) with black curly hair and hazel eyes and 5'10" tall. Two of his brothers Coleman and Thomas E. and his Uncle Shadrach, also joined the Confederate States of America Army. Records also show their enlistment. Ironically as it may seem, all four were eventually captured by Union Forces and their releases are recorded. Records of all four of these young men are found in the Civil War records.

Coleman G. Johnson also joined the confederate army and received his $50.00 payment. Coleman was only 16 years of age when he joined the C.S.A. in Monroe.

In 1863, Union records show that John Evan Johnson was captured and became a prisoner of the Union Army. There is no mention of where he was captured although other records of his brothers and Uncle also show where they were captured as well as where they were held and released. He was later pardoned by the Union Commander and released from the prisoner of war camp near Monroe, Louisiana in July 1863. He had signed a statement declaring that he would no longer participate in the war for the Confederates.

Shortly after his release and pardon, John Evan Johnson again joined the CSA and again received his $50.00 payment. This time he was in Company 6 of Grays 28th Louisiana Infantry. On May 27, 1865, records show that John Evan Johnson was again a prisoner of the Union Army and was again pardoned and released.

Shadrach Johnson was also a confederate soldier. He joined the CSA army and was in Company I, 31st regiment Louisiana Infantry and taken prisoner at the battle of Vicksburg. Shadrach was then released by a Maj. Duncan in Vicksburg on July 9, 1863, following the surrender of Confederate forces in Vicksburg, where they were besieged and starved by the Union army until they surrendered on July 4, 1863. Shadrach then reenlisted and was again captured near Vienna, Louisiana on April 1, 1864. Again, he was released from the Union Army's Prison Camp near New Orleans one year later, on June 10, 1865.

Coleman Johnson, John Evans brother joined the CSA army and was in Company D, First Louisiana Reserve. He would have been only a teenager at the beginning of the war. He was captured and became a prisoner of the Union Army near Natchitoches, Louisiana and was released in a prisoner exchange at Natchitoches, Louisiana on June 17, 1865. Records do not show the place of his capture but only his enlistment and his release.

Another son of Zattie, Thomas F. Johnson also joined the Confederate States of America Army and as did his brothers re-ceived the $50.00 payment. Thomas F. Johnson was in Company F, 27th Regiment, Louisiana. He, too, was captured by Union Forces in Vicksburg, Mississippi on July 4, 1863. He remained a prisoner of the Union forces until he was released in April 1865, in a prisoner exchange in Shreveport, Louisiana. It is not known for certain, but surely believed that the two relatives, Uncle Shadrach and nephew Thomas E. were aware that each was in Vicksburg with the Confederate army during the battle and siege. Why Thomas E. was held as a prisoner but his Uncle was released is unknown. He remained in the Union prisoner camps for two years.

CHAPTER 16

———◆———

AFTER THE WAR WAS OVER John Evan Johnson traveled back to Winn Parish, Louisiana to be with his family and remained there for almost one year. He then decided to move his family to Monroe, Louisiana. While they were in Monroe another child was born to him and his wife Mary Catherine. This was a daughter who died shortly afterward.

News was received that all Confederate war veterans were eligible to receive a veteran's war grant of 160 acres in Arkansas. John Evan quickly applied for this land grant because he was familiar with this area of Arkansas. His family had already been in the Warren, and Moro Bay, Bradley County, Arkansas area. After John Evan received his 160 acres of land he and his family moved back to Moro Bay, Bradley County where he would remain until his death.

John Evan quickly seized upon the land opportunities that he suddenly found himself privy to. He began purchasing the land granted to other Confederate Veterans. Perhaps three of these purchases were from his relatives, Uncle Shadrach and brother Coleman, and his brother Thomas F. Johnson, who had also served in the Confederate Army. They too would have received this notice or would have been aware of the available land for their service in the Confederate Army. They applied and received the 160-acre land grant but did not desire to move from the Winn Parish,

Louisiana area, so they were possibly the ones who sold their land grants to John Evan.

Regardless of who he purchased the additional land from, John Evan became a large land owner in Bradley County, Arkansas. The land held a wealth of large, virgin, merchantable timber. In order to clear the land, John Evan began to market the timber as he cleared the land for farming. The result was that he and his family amassed a very comfortable living through his logging and timber operations. The family has in their possession several photos of the logging operations in the Bradley County area. He and his wife had another child, born in Bradley County in December 1866. This child was a son named:

****Hubert Lee Johnson.

We will now list the children of John Evan and his wife in the order of their birth.

****William Jasper Johnson born in Winn Parish, Louisiana on 05/23/1859
A daughter was born in Monroe, Louisiana in 1865, but died shortly after birth.
****Hubert Lee Johnson, born in December 1866, in Bradley County, Arkansas

Other children born there were a daughter, Mary Catherine 1868,

Willie Francis, a daughter, was born in 1872. This daughter died at the age of eleven and is buried in Marsden Cemetery in Bradley County, and
Martha Ella Johnson born February 22, 1873.
Another child was born in Arkansas but also died shortly after birth.

Although there are ten children known to have been born to John Evan and his wife Mary Katherine, there are three that cannot be accounted for. We do know of two deaths of their children when they were young or infants but the third is not available in records which tend to indicate that this other child also died at birth or an early age and was not recorded in the census.

John Evan received word in 1878 that his father Zattie Johnson had died in Winn Parish, Louisiana. He was buried in Oak Grove Cemetery in Olla, Winn Parish, Louisiana. This cemetery would eventually have a large Johnson contingency buried there over the next one hundred years. Today this cemetery is inaccessible to the public because several hundred acres surrounding the cemetery has been purchased by a hunting club and is fenced off and posted as no trespassing with locked gates leading into the property, thus, closing off access to the cemetery.

After Zattie Johnson died, his wife Margaret Anna lived with her son Shadrach (Confederate War Veteran) until her death a short time later. She is also buried in the Shady Grove Cemetery. Another son of Zattie and Margaret Anna, Coleman, also a Confederate War Veteran, died in 1884 and was buried near his family in Shady Grove Cemetery.

After his father, Zattie, died in Winn Parish, Louisiana, John Evan would never return to Winn Parish. Instead he remained in Bradley County, maintaining his timber and farming operations. John Evan Johnson died July 8, 1899. John Evan's wife, Mary Katherine filed a claim for a Civil War Veterans Pension in 1899, claiming her husband, who died on July 8th, 1899, had died from **"Being completely worn out from old age"**. He was 69 years old. Mary Katherine died February 2, 1916 and is buried beside her husband in Marsden Cemetery in Bradley County, Arkansas.

———

CHAPTER 17

WILLIAM JASPER JOHNSON, WHO WAS born shortly before his father John Evan joined the Confederate Army, was first raised in Louisiana until he was six years of age. Shortly after his father returned from the Civil War they moved to Monroe, Louisiana where they lived for about one year. They went temporarily to Bradley County, Arkansas for about one year then back to Monroe, Louisiana. When he was about ten years of age, in 1869, the family moved permanently to Bradley County, Arkansas.

William Jasper Johnson, the first-born son of John Evan and his wife Mary Katherine became a logger and farmer as was his dad. Bradley County is near the Ouachita River which flows from west central Arkansas into central Louisiana. This area of rich bottom land produced some of Arkansas best timber and fertile farm land. William Jasper met a young woman from "The Other Side of The River" in Union County, named Martha Jane Carter. They were married in El Dorado, Arkansas on June 23, 1879. Her parents were Julia (Branch) Black and John Washington Carter. These are names of two of the families that were mentioned earlier, as early settlers with Zattie and Jeremiah Johnson, in the southern Arkansas area. There were several connections through marriage between some of these earlier Arkansas residents' who had moved there from Mississippi.

After their marriage, William Jasper and Mary Jane began a family with five children being born between 1880-1887. Although the family was doing well in the timber and farming business, William became involved in a situation in 1890, in Warren Arkansas that would change his life completely and create a problem of survival for his large family.

Records and newspaper accounts from the State newspaper, "<u>The Arkansas Gazette</u>", record the following information.

In August 1890, a young Negro man was arrested and taken to the Warren, Arkansas jail located at the Bradley County courthouse in Warren. His arrest was for accusations that he had made improper advances toward a young white woman and possible assault of her and later assaulted another woman.

Below is an actual report obtained from records of the Arkansas Gazette

A BLACK BRUTE LYNCHED FOR A CRIMINAL ASSAULT UPON A YOUNG WHITE WOMAN
Captured by the Officers, But Taken by an Armed Posse and Swung Up in the Public Square at Warren
Special to The Arkansas Gazette
Arkansas City August 11---Last Friday morning a negro boy, about 20 years of age, (actual age was around fifteen or sixteen) named William Beavers, living with Mr. Abernathy near Warren, Bradley County, Arkansas, assaulted and attempted to outrage Miss Inez Abernathy while the young woman was gathering eggs on her fathers' lot. She fought the brute off and screamed, bringing her mother from the house to her assistance. The negro fled without having accomplished his purpose.

That evening the brute met a young negro girl near Mr. Sutton's plantation. He was unsuccessful this time also.

Friday night, news of the fiends' assault upon Miss Abernathy becoming known, and a posse of men was organized to arrest him. Sunday evening about dark he was captured by Sheriff Watson and Deputy out a few miles from Warren. The officers started to jail with their prisoner, but were met on the road by an armed mob of eight or ten men, who took Beavers from Watson, locked the Sheriff and his deputy up in the jail and swung the negro to a limb. This morning the body of the would-be rapist was found dangling from the end of a rope on the public square.

On August 13, 1890, an additional report was printed by the Arkansas Gazette and later transcribed in 1892 in a follow up story that included William's brother, Henry Jr.

You will notice some incorrect dates that were placed in the articles which were later transcribed from several different sources, and make the combination of these reports somewhat confusing.

In 1880 census, William Beavers and his brother, Junior, who was two years older (presumably Henry) were living in Pennington Township of Bradley County, Arkansas, with their parents, Henry and Lorenda Beavers and several other siblings. Henry Beavers Senior was in his thirties and was a farmer. Both brothers were described by the <u>Gazette</u> as "Brutes".

According to the <u>Gazette</u>, by 1890 William Beavers, stated to be, supposedly twenty years of age (dates are inaccurately transcribed; Census places his age as fifteen or sixteen at this time) was living near Warren, Arkansas with J.H. Abernathy, a Confederate Veteran and prominent farmer. On the morning of August 8th,

Beavers encountered Mr. Abernathy's daughter, Inez, while she was gathering eggs from the family farm. He assaulted her, and attempted to "outrage her". She screamed and alerted her mother. Beavers fled and later attempted to assault a young Negro (*changed to read African American*) Girl near "Mr. Sutton's plantation." This Mr. Sutton is probably David W. Sutton who was listed as a prominent farmer in Bradley County.

Area residents learned of the assault on Inez Abernathy that night and formed a posse. William Beavers was captured a few miles from Warren on August 10, 1890. When Sheriff William Rufus Watson and four assistants attempted to take him to a cell, a group of men (first reported to be eight or ten men) seized the sheriff from behind and took away his keys. According to the Gazette, "Sheriff Watson and two of his deputies were then forcibly carried upstairs and locked in the jail, and two more were taken under guard and carried to the foundry." Although the sheriff and his deputies shouted out from the jail, no one heard them for several hours. The <u>Gazette</u> stated, "No blame is attached to the Sheriff, as he was overpowered, and unable even to give an alarm…He says the party, as far as he could tell, were all masked, and recognitions were impossible."

At this point, William Beavers knew what was about to take place and began to plead with the mob to spare his life.

Beavers was hanged from a nearby tree, near the Warren County Courthouse and Jail. The <u>Gazette</u> goes on to call William Beavers a "troublesome fellow", who "had been for a year or two a terror to the women and children". He was already under bond for another assault on a colored girl, and would probably have gone to the Penitentiary for that offence, had he not been so summarily disposed of for his last act.

In February 1892, (one and one half years later) William's brother Henry, who was two years older than William, was accused of assaulting Chloe Wright near Wilmar. According to the Byrne family tree, Chloe Wright was the daughter of Drew County farmer Andrew Jackson Wright and his wife, Eliza. Chloe was about seventeen or eighteen at the time of the alleged assault.

The <u>Gazette</u> reported on February 9, 1892, that the assault on Chloe Wright occurred between Wilmar and Alice Station (Drew County) at 9:00 a.m. on February 8th. Although this initial report identifies Beavers as "Jim Beavers", and refers to him as the brother of "Jeff Beavers" who had been lynched the previous year (actually, August 10, 1890 or one and one half years). Census records do not seem to reflect these names used here but they do reflect William and Henry Jr. Research indicates that the two Beavers brothers who were hanged were indeed William in August of 1890, and then in February 1892, his brother, Henry was lynched.

The <u>New York Sun</u> reported on Henry Beavers' murder on February 9, 1892. Chloe was described as "attractive and popular", and her father as "a farmer and an influential citizen." According to the Sun's report, Chloe was halfway between her house and the nearest neighbor's when she was "met in the public road by Beavers, who made improper proposals. Then he seized and threw her to the ground, holding her by the throat and choking her almost into unconsciousness." Chloe fought back and told Beavers that her mother was coming, and he fled. Chloe was apparently badly injured, but she was expected to recover.

News of the attack quickly spread. The <u>Sun</u> stated, "In less than half an hour, horsemen armed with pistols and clubs were scouring the woods in every direction." Around 1:00 p.m., they discovered Beavers walking with his mother along the railroad tracks toward Wilmar. When approached, he did not resist and was taken into town, where he was quickly surrounded by a mob of 150 people. They took him to the Wright home, where

Chloe recognized him and where he supposedly confessed. The crowd then took Beavers back into town, "where they paraded him through the principal thoroughfares." They then forced him to carry a rope to a tree in the woods. There the rope was thrown over a limb, and Beavers was put on a horse with the noose around his neck. When the horse began to move, "Beavers was left dangling in the air. Before the body ceased to vibrate a volley of shots rang out and it was perforated with no fewer than sixty bullets."

The Sun reported that Henry Beavers was only seventeen and was the brother of William Beavers, "who was hanged to a tree in the court yard at this place one and one half years ago, for an attempted assault upon a young white girl."

As written by the Gazette, the grand jury "composed of our best citizens," refused even to consider the coroner's report on Henry Beavers' death, refusing "to investigate or even read the contents within."

Note: The most accurate accounts of these two men would be that William Beavers was fifteen or sixteen years of age at his death and his brother Henry Beavers would have been eighteen or nineteen at the time of his death.

Note: Chloe Wright did recover from the reported attack. On April 10, 1894, she married Thomas Gregory Byrne. By 1900, they were living in Wilmar with their three children. Chloe Byrne died in 1912 at the age of thirty-seven.

William Jasper Johnson was believed to be the leader of the lynch mob that hanged William Beavers on August 10, 1890. Below is another record obtained from a source listing Negro Men hung in Arkansas in the late 1800s. The young negro man who was hung in Warren, Bradley County, Arkansas in 1890 appears in this document along with the actual date of his death by hanging from a lynch mob.

8-10-1890	William Beavers	Bradley	black male	rape
1-1-1890	(unreported)	Phillips	black male	complicity in murder

One can go to the internet and read about thousands of lynchings and murders of mostly black men during the late 1800s and early 1900s.

During this dark period in U.S. history, and especially in the south, we find that most lynchings occurred between 1890 and 1920. Those persons were almost always exclusively black men being lynched by white vigilante groups and occurred almost always, yet not exclusively in the south. These lynchings also included white men who tried to protect or defend the black men being accused of various crimes. Some of these crimes that they were accused of were often, for merely looking at or speaking to a white woman, and then reports were often exaggerated and got out of control. In many of these instances, these men were innocent victims found guilty of simply making a friendly greeting.

There were also some women hanged as well as many young black teenagers. There were many lynchings reported in Georgia and in Mississippi from 1870, and as late as 1950.

One student from Berea College wrote the following statistics.

From 1882-1968, 4,743 lynchings occurred in the United States. Of these people that were lynched 3,446 were black. The blacks lynched accounted for 72.7% of the people lynched. These numbers seem large, but it is known that not all the lynchings were ever recorded. Out of the 4,743-people lynched only 1,297 white people were lynched. That is only 27.3%. Many of the whites lynched were lynched for helping the black or being anti-lynching and even for domestic crimes.

The best account of what followed is that William Jasper Johnson who was believed to be the leader of the lynch mob, immediately left the Arkansas area for Winn Parish, Louisiana, out of fear that he and his lynch mob would be prosecuted. His method of travel is not known but is believed to have been south through Monroe, Louisiana, then south to Winn Parish by horse. He could have also taken a route down the Ouachita River by boat to Monroe then by horse to Winn Parish. We only know that his departure was in haste and that he eventually ended up in Winn Parish.

William stayed a few days with his grandfather, Zattie Johnson, and other relatives in Winn Parish, then hurriedly left for the Big Thicket area of East Texas, a few miles west of Winn Parish. This would have put him in or near Jasper, Texas where it was reported that other relatives now lived. He then teamed up with a nephew also named Zattie Johnson after his grandfather. The younger Zattie was the son of Shadrach, Johnson, and the grandson of his namesake Zattie Johnson. Shadrach and John Evan Johnson were the sons of the elder Zattie Johnson. After hiding out in the Big Thicket area of East Texas for some time, he and his nephew then made their way to Houston, Texas, before deciding to move back north, to Dallas, Texas. They then left the Dallas area and returned to Winn Parish for a few days.

The year is now 1894 and William is still on the run from authorities thinking they were in pursuit and certainly feeling guilty of his crime. No information nor evidence was known of the authorities pursuing William and the other members of his lynch mob. Nor were there any reports in the Arkansas Gazette of such pursuits that we could locate. This does not mean that the men who assisted in the hanging were not questioned but nevertheless William Jasper Johnson spent years running in fear and making every effort to evade authorities and answer for his crime.

The next travel for William Jasper, as he evaded authorities is reported to be from Winn Parish to the state of Missouri. This move would take William and his nephew back through Arkansas. He and his nephew made a quick stop in Bradley County, Arkansas to check on his family who he had not seen for four years. Martha Jane was now dependent on her father-in-law, John Evan Johnson and her father, John Washington Carter, for the care of her and William's children.

After this brief, but secret stop in Bradley County, the two men reportedly made their way to Missouri and spent a short time there. He had obviously been informed and knew that some of his family was in Mississippi and he had discovered that one brother, Hubert Lee Johnson had moved to Sipsey, Alabama, near Birmingham. William Jasper and his cousin Zattie Johnson made their way through southern Missouri and then into Alabama to another relative's home. This relative was his brother, Hubert Lee. It was reported that William showed up in Alabama and remained near his brother Hubert Lee, for almost three years. Hubert Lee was married and now had three children in Alabama and a stepdaughter. Hubert Lee later abandoned his wife and children in Alabama for reasons unknown. He left this area in 1900 to return to Bradley County, Arkansas. We will include this brother Hubert Lee Johnson and his interesting life, in a later part of this narrative.

From this point in time, namely 1899-1900, we do not know what happened to William Jasper Johnson, nor is there any further information of his running mate, the younger Zattie Johnson. There are no census reports or other documents that can be located that include these two names. Perhaps when his brother Hubert Lee went back to Arkansas, they secretly made their way back to that area and he remained there under an assumed name. The younger Zattie, probably would have returned to Winn Parish, Louisiana or to Jasper, Texas to be with his immediate family.

We only know that William Jasper's wife, Martha Jane continued to live near her father and mother-in-law, raising her and Williams's children. Martha Jane died in 1922 and is buried in Marsden Bradley County Cemetery with numerous other Johnsons.

Somehow it was always known what William Jasper Johnson's travels were and where and how long he was in different areas. So, there had to be a connection somewhere for this information to be known. True each of the relatives would probably have been told by him, where he had been and perhaps even where he was going after each brief visit. It is a definite that his brother Hubert Lee would have known of his travels through 1896-1900 and could have passed this information on to his other family members in Arkansas.

We do know that William Jasper Johnson was never prosecuted for the hanging in Warren County of the young black man, William Beavers, that he was accused of lynching. Our conclusion is that after his brother Hubert Lee moved back to Bradley County, Arkansas, William Jasper later returned and reunited with his family. He probably, after ten years, had assumed another identity and secretly lived out his remaining years in that area where he was raised. He would have been forty-one years of age in nineteen hundred. Perhaps the authorities even knew that he had returned but as was common in lynching's cases in the south, they never intended to prosecute him and allowed him to live without any efforts to punish him or the other members of the lynch mob.

Then we can also look at the Sun newspaper report which used a report from the <u>Arkansas Gazette</u>, and what they stated, concerning the death of Henry Beavers. The Gazette reported "a grand jury was selected of outstanding citizens and refused to use the coroner's report to pursue anyone in the death of Henry". Perhaps this was also the outcome of the earlier lynching of Henry's brother, William Beavers. They refused to even read the coroner's report concerning the facts that caused his death.

Let's take a brief detour from the narrative and fast forward to the 1970s for the purpose of relating the following story.

One of William Jasper Johnson's sons, was named Robert Cisroe Johnson, who also had a son named Rufus Norman Johnson.

Rufus Norman Johnson spent the last years of his life trying to trace the Johnson family's history. Rufus Norman was doing all of this by actually visiting individual family members and physically checking Archives and Court House records. He spent hundreds of hours if not thousands of hours as well as traveling thousands of miles talking to relatives, getting statements and photos. He would then follow those bits of information and obtain additional information. He finally put the gathered information into a family history.

This was in the late 1960s and early 1970s when these facts were not obtainable on the computer with the ease in which they are accessible today. Included below is an article that appeared in the Arkansas newspaper of Rufus Norman Johnson.

Man in Half Moon plans
to produce own electricity

BY MARK CARNOPIS
Democrat Conway Bureau

HALF MOON - For more than three years, Rufus Norman Johnson has lived without electricity in this small Van Buren County community. Now, he is making plans to produce his own.

Johnson, 58, said last week he was working on two power sources for his cabin - a roof of solar cells and a water wheel.

"I don't want power line electricity ... no way," Johnson said of utility companies. "I'm the happiest man in the world without them."

The lights and stove in the small rock and wood cabin he built for $800 in 1982 operate on butane gas. He recently junked a butane icebox, his second, after "it just blowed out."

Has a cool cellar

Heat is provided by a large wood-burning stove, and he said the cellar where he sleeps stays cool during the summer.

Johnson's decision to do without electricity was based on economics and a confrontation with the area power company.

It was in August 1981 that Johnson moved to a small house trailer in this community of about 300 residents eight miles east of Botkinberg. Johnson called the Petit Jean Electric Cooperative Corp. and asked for a hookup.

Home not 'permanent'

Because his home didn't qualify as a permanent residence, officials demanded a $1,000 deposit to install two electric poles and connect Johnson to the system. Johnson was unwilling to pay that or a $750 deposit arranged as a compromise.

A flurry of letters to elected officials resulted in Johnson's filing a complaint with the state Public Service Commission. Johnson said the PSC told him that he could get electricity but would have to pay about $215 for the cost of running the power line to his home. Johnson still refused to pay.

Finally, the utility provided him with a hookup without cost in January 1982. Four months later, he moved to his cabin and decided it was too much trouble to get hooked up to the electric company again.

Life isn't difficult

Johnson said adjusting to a life without electricity wasn't difficult. He lives on less than $400 a month in disability benefits. He proudly claimed that $25 worth of butane gas purchased last spring was still keeping his lights and stove burning.

Johnson said he probably would have gotten electricity if any of his 11 children or numerous grandchildren were living with him. As it is, Johnson said he can do without television and other devices needing electricity. He said he became interested in making his own electricity after reading at a library about different methods to do so.

During a tour of the grounds outside his cabin, Johnson pointed with pride to the site where he will build his steel water wheel. Water will be piped from a pond about 300 yards away. Johnson hopes the system, expected to cost about $1,000, will produce enough electricity to run a refrigerator and four 100-watt light bulbs.

Johnson was also planning to install solar panels to produce electricity. He expected both generating systems to be operating by spring.

Independence 'satisfying'

Johnson said his independence from the electric company has been satisfying, and he urged others follow his example.

"If there are older people out there with no children and don't care about television, this is the best lifestyle you can have," Johnson explained. "And you can live just about anywhere for it."

Johnson said if more people were self-reliant, the price of electricity would go down because electric companies would find ways of making their electricity cheaper to win back customers.

Arkansas

SELF-RELIANT MAN — Rufus Norman Johnson of Half Moon sits at the entrance his $800 cabin. Below. Johnson shows off scrap metal from which he plans to make a water wheel to produce electricity.

Arkansas Democrat/Mark Cornelison

——————

****HUBERT LEE JOHNSON WAS BORN in 1866, in Moro Bay, Bradley County, Arkansas. This was the second living son of John Evan and Mary Catherine. Hubert Lee was accustomed to the hard work demands of farming and logging. He was a part of his father's successful farming and timber business as was his older brother William Jasper. As was required of almost all farming operations in the south, the children carried a lot of responsibility in the working aspect of the farm.

In 1888, Hubert Lee married a lady named Mary Halley House-Raborn, who was born in Wilmington, North Carolina. Mary Halley had been married before and was the widow of Henry Raborn. They had one child together before her husband Henry died. They named this daughter Laura Raborn. Laura was born in 1885. The House family also had moved to the Arkansas area when there were a large number of new families desiring to claim some of the farm and timber land that was being offered as a grant to new families. Mary Halley's father, Martin House, was born in Wilmington. North Carolina. She had a brother named Henry Clarence House who had married Hubert Lee's sister, Mary Ella Johnson in Arkansas.

On July 7, 1889, a son was born in Marsden, Arkansas to Hubert Lee and Mary Halley Johnson. He was named William Lee after his father and uncle. They then had a daughter named Mierta who was born in Marsden, Arkansas in October 10, 1890. She died in 1935, in Alabama, never having been married nor having children.

Having some historical ties to the Alabama area, namely Dallas County, Hubert Lee and Mary Halley left Moro Bay around 1890-1891 and moved to Sipsey, Alabama. Dallas County is near Birmingham, Alabama. Another son named Hubert Canal "Pink" Johnson was born there in 1892. These two brothers were always close to each other and where one went the other would also go.

It is not known why, but in 1900, Hubert Lee left his wife, Mary Halley Johnson and their children and returned to Bradley County, Arkansas. We know that this was also about the time that William Jasper Johnson who had left the Arkansas area on the run from authorities had appeared in Alabama and lived close to Hubert Lee and his family from 1896-1900. After Hubert Lee left for Arkansas, Mary Halley Johnson remained in Sipsey, Alabama and raised the children. She died in 1910 and was buried in Sipsey, Alabama.

Perhaps the reason for returning to Moro Bay, Arkansas in early 1900 was the news that his father John Evan Johnson had died in July 1899. Since his father was a well-respected farmer and timber man, there would be a need to return and make himself available for the care of the family property. Whatever the reason we do not know. We only know that something happened which changed and controlled the future of Hubert Lee. There is no information as to how the property of John Evan was divided or if the wife of John Evan sold the property. We do know that after John Evan died, his wife filed for a Civil War Veterans pension and received it until she died in 1916, in Bradley County.

Speculation could be that Hubert Lee and his father John Evan, had a falling out (a family quarrel) and this was the reason Hubert Lee had left Moro Bay, Arkansas for Alabama in the first place. When his father died, he returned to the Moro Bay area expecting to be one of the heirs to his father's property only to discover that the possible and probable feud was long standing and he was not an heir to the family property after all. We also know that Hubert Lee was always struggling financially, from the time he returned to Moro Bay.

There is no evidence that he was written out of his father's will, but circumstances indicate that this was definitely the case. Even when his mother died in 1916, there was no evidence that Hubert Lee was the benefactor of any of his father's property. Hubert Lee was never an owner of property in the Warren County area except the small plot where he eventually built a home.

The above was certainly a probability since Hubert Lee never received any inheritance of record. We do know that he would have two families. One remained in Alabama and another would begin in Bradley County, Arkansas, after he left his wife and children in Alabama and returned to Warren County. Why he never returned to Alabama and his wife Mary Halley and his children will always be a mystery. In the years to follow, it would seem that the two families would always be biologically connected but for the most part, geographically separated.

The sons of the Alabama family would eventually move to North Carolina and the other family would always be in Deep South states with very little interaction within the extended family. Zattie May (Jack) and his older brother were an exception. Jack and his brother Roy Lee were always in contact with Hubert Canal and William Lee Johnson. The two half-brothers of Jack and Roy Lee lived in and around Greensboro and Roy Lee moved there in the early 1940s and remained near his half-brothers for the rest of their lives. Jack was always in touch with the brothers and had on two occasions moved his family to Greensboro to live.

When he returned to Bradley County, Arkansas, Hubert Lee met and married Elizabeth "Lizzy" Glaze Horn who was from Louisiana. Elizabeth had been married to Paul Horn and had one daughter named Evelyn "Eva" Bernice Horn, before she was widowed. Hubert Lee and Elizabeth had seven sons:

Roy Lee Johnson was born in Marsden, Arkansas October 24th, 1906
Troy Johnson, born in May 1909
George W. Johnson born June 12, 1910
****Zattie May "Jack" Johnson born May 1, 1911
Hazel, born in 1916
Twin sons named Eller and Almer Johnson were born January 8, 1918.

After the twin boys were born, Elizabeth "Lizzy" Johnson never recovered from complications from the birth of their twin sons. She died in April 1918. Eller, one of the twin boys, was never healthy and finally succumbed shortly after his mother on July 8, 1918, leaving Hubert Lee, the father of the remaining six young children, full responsibility for their care.

In trying to explain Hubert Lee's past actions and those that are forthcoming are without any definitive first-hand knowledge. We do know that there were a lot of tragic things happening between 1890-1922, in the lives of the Johnson family:

- William Jasper had been on the run from authorities after the hanging of the young black man, in which he was believed to be a participant:
- John Evan, Hubert Lee's father, had died in 1899;
- Hubert Lee left his wife and children in Alabama in 1900;
- His wife, Mary Halley, whom he had left in Alabama, died in 1910. Their three children were now on their own.
- His mother Mary Katherine, died in 1916;
- Hubert Lee's wife Elizabeth, died in 1918;
- His twin son died in 1918;
- His house burned to the ground in 1921:
- His children were then separated to adoption and foster care.

This would have been a huge amount of tragedy for anyone.

Roy Lee was the oldest at home when his mother Elizabeth died and he was now twelve years of age. The father, Hubert Lee had just built a new home not far from the Ouachita River in Moro Bay. He continued to care for the young children with the assistance of his stepdaughter Evelyn (Eva) Horn. She was only 16 at the time of her mother's death. She married shortly afterwards to a man named Ellis Webb and they were never able to have children. Evelyn continued to try and help her stepfather care for her siblings.

Hubert Lee's final decision was the only reasonable plan (as he could view it) that he could come up with. He would need to place his children up for adoption and/or foster his children out to relatives. A young family by the name of Temple, made arrangements to adopt the young surviving twin boy, Almer. Roy Lee being the oldest of the children went to live with his half-sister Evelyn, as did George. Relatives helped to care for the other boys, Troy and Hazel while Zattie May (Jack) refused to leave his father. The older sister, and young bride, Evelyn continued to help in the care of the children and struggled to keep them together.

Two years after his wife died Hubert Lee met and married another lady named Ollie Smith. With all the struggles of caring for a now divided family Hubert Lee, his new wife Ollie and his son Zattie May, who was now eleven years of age and had refused to leave his father, decided on another plan.

In 1921 a fire had started in the Hubert Lee Johnson home and they were unable to put the fire out. The home that was only a few years old and had been built by Hubert Lee was destroyed. Hubert Lee would contend that the fire was not an accident but was intentionally set but who had intentionally set the fire has never been known. If Hubert Lee had suspicions or knew the individual, it was never revealed or the information was forgotten over time. It seemed that disaster would not leave the family alone. Now without a home and struggling to take care of his young family, who had been dispersed to live with different families, Hubert Lee began to contemplate his next move in his life's struggle.

CHAPTER 19

———◆———

HUBERT LEE'S NEW PLAN BEGAN to unfold. Now feeling that his children were cared for, or perhaps again running from his respon-
sibilities, he began construction of a small raft or barge, with the
remaining and salvageable timbers from the burned home and
other lumber he could find. The construction was on the banks
of the Ouachita River at Moro Bay, Arkansas. The final product
resembled a one room cabin on a raft.

His plan was that he would push off from the banks of the
Ouachita River and let the current carry him, his new wife and remaining son to places unknown. Hubert Lee was aware of the city
of Monroe about one hundred plus miles downriver that promised
the hope of a new start in life. This would also put him nearer
his grandfather and other family members who resided in Winn
Parish. However there had been very little or limited interaction
between the Winn Parish Zattie Johnsons and his son John Evan
who had been separated since the 1860s.

Perhaps he hoped he could leave the multitude of hardship
in Bradley County, Arkansas, land somewhere downstream and
then begin that new life. Monroe was one of the prospective places
where he hoped to find a job and start a new life. In the spring
of 1922, the family that was now down to three, placed all their
meager belongings and household items on the now completed
raft or barge and pushed off to someplace, at that time, uncertain

and unknown. Hubert Lee hoped this would somehow change the struggles that he had faced for several years. The raft voyage would eventually carry the now family of three, over two hundred fifty miles down the Ouachita River.

As the river current took control of the raft, Hubert Lee and Zattie now used homemade paddles and poles to help control the raft as the unpredictable Ouachita River took control of their destiny. The struggle was to control the raft and prevent the currents and often swirling waters from causing the raft to spin or become entangled in the floating debris on the river and perhaps disastrously damaging the manmade craft.

They had very little money, very little food and only enough household items to sustain their trip. They did not know how long it would take to arrive in Monroe. Their only hope was that as the current took them by other small communities on the Ouachita, they could find enough work to refurbish their meager food supply.

Several weeks later, after several short stops, they finally arrived at Monroe, Louisiana. They managed to get their raft to shore and began to look for work and the beginning of a new future. Zattie May (Jack), who was now eleven years of age, also worked with odd jobs. They were only able to find temporary work that lasted only a few days but still enough to buy supplies.

After struggling to find permanent work in Monroe and being unsuccessful they decided to again push their raft out into the Ouachita and again be at the mercy of the Ouachita River. He had been told of another town farther down the Ouachita River that was said to have a lot of work. The small town was Jonesville, Louisiana, which was only a few miles from Natchez, Mississippi. In the Jonesville vicinity, there were several large plantations, large forests of timber and several sawmills.

The farming belt in that area of Louisiana stretched from Jonesville as far east as the Mississippi River and to the north-northeast. To the north and west around this farming area was a large timber and forest area. Other large timber and forest areas were present in this river bottom area of Louisiana. These farming and timber industry were an economical boost to the Jonesville economy.

Because of the large timber growth, there were stated to be several saw mills and Hubert Lee was all too familiar with the timber and logging business. He had been raised in a family who had large timber on their property and was familiar with logging and sawmill work. Word had spread that there was a lot of work there and so the prospects of a permanent job and a new future were believed to be a real possibility.

Once again, they floated down the river with the current as their only means of propulsion and struggling to control the raft in the currents by poles and homemade paddles. Each bend in the river brought into view another obstacle or danger that they never knew existed. Some were logs or fallen trees or sharp bends that presented strong currents and caused the raft to quickly head toward bushes and possibly entangle the family's raft. The ride was never a time of easy slowly drifting in which they could relax. Danger may lie around the next bend.

The distance by river was about one hundred forty miles from Monroe to Jonesville. They had been very dependent on the homemade barge/raft now for over a month. They were now sure that they could depend on this floating mass of timbers and scrap lumber to carry them to their next destination. During their float down the river they would struggle often with the raft drifting into bushes or limbs where they would struggle to free themselves and continue their float down the river.

Zattie May Johnson had never liked his name even if it had been a name of several of his ancestors and the name of his great grandfather. He had wanted to be called Jack and he was determined to drop the given name of Zattie May Johnson and be known only as Jack Johnson, with no middle name necessary; only Jack Johnson.

So, from early in his teenage years Zattie May Johnson became Jack Johnson and he would claim this name for the rest of his life. Some of his immediate family members never knew that his given name had been different from that of Jack. For some, this information would become known only when the family ancestry was traced many years later.

The three occupants of the raft would often struggle to land the raft when they saw a farmhouse. Since it was spring and early summer there was always the hopes of a garden full of fresh vegetables and perhaps the family living there would share with them. They were always amazed at the hospitality of the strangers that they met on their journey to their next destination. The families, it seemed, were always willing to share.

Many times, they struggled with the spring rains, which were often torrential. Any time there was a heavy rain north of where they were floating, they were sure that the run-off would be deposited into the Ouachita River. They also knew that it was just a matter of time before the Ouachita would begin to rise and the currents becoming more swift. This was always a danger. It was too dangerous to try to float with the rising water and the increased debris floating in the river. With no means of propulsion other than the rivers current and with only strength and determination from the three occupants to control the raft, Hubert Lee and his now small family would wait it out until the dangers were past.

When there was a heavy rain in the area they would tie the raft to shore and wait it out, hoping that the river would not create undue delays in their journey and they could again navigate the currents. They would always tie up to the bank of the river at night and make a campfire to prepare their meals. The dangers of remaining floating on the raft or being on the river at night were just too great with the unknown route of the river nor knowing of the hazards that could be around the next bend. Sometimes they would make their beds near the campfire or sometimes they would tie the raft up and remain on it, to spend the night while battling the insects, which were plentiful in the river area this time of year.

After several days of floating, Hubert Lee, his wife Ollie and son, Jack, finally arrived at a junction on the Ouachita River where two other rivers flowed into the Ouachita River. One narrow river flowed from the northeast into the Ouachita and was named the Tensas River. Then just south of that junction and on the opposite side of the Ouachita was another river, also narrow compared to the Ouachita. The other river flowed from the west was named Little River. Little River is only a few miles long, thus the name. On the west side of the river and at the junction of the Little River was the town they had been looking for. The city of Jonesville. At this junction, the name of the river changed. The river became wider and it now became known as the Black River which continued to flow southwest to join the Red River.

The Red River flowed from the northwest and stretched thirteen hundred miles, at one point flowing from almost due west separating the Texas and Oklahoma borders. This was the Red River that was listed in the Indian Treaties as the southern boundary of the designated Indian Nations land in the Oklahoma territory. It begins in the Texas panhandle and flows almost due east separating Texas and Oklahoma Then through Louisiana until it joins the Atchafalaya and Mississippi Rivers in southern Louisiana. It was the recognized boundary line for the state of Texas and Oklahoma. The Black River ends at the junction with the Red River. The Red River continued flowing south-south east until it joined the mighty Mississippi River.

The trusty raft had endured the trip that had now taken almost two months and had traversed the Ouachita for over two hundred fifty miles. The Johnson 's tied their raft up at the bank near the town of Jonesville. The town stretched from the banks of the Ouachita and its banks to the Little River as its other boundary. City streets ran down to the riverfront. Docks were both on the Little River and the Ouachita.

The docks were used to load boats with lumber from the several sawmills and to load cotton and other farm products for shipment. These products were shipped as far south as Baton Rouge and New Orleans. Because the town was close to the Mississippi River to the East and the city of Natchez, Mississippi, many of the products were transported by rail and wagons to the Mississippi river at Natchez for shipment both north to Vicksburg and even farther and south on the Mississippi River to Baton Rouge and New Orleans.

Hubert Lee and Jack immediately set out to look for work. Hubert Lee found work at one of the sawmills. There was a heavy growth of Ash Timber in the area and one of the mills produced nothing but Ash lumber and materials used for baseball bats as well as other Ash lumber products. Jack who had just turned twelve years of age in May, also began working at one of the Ash Mills. His formal education, which was already limited, was now over.

Hubert Lee could now begin to try and reestablish his life. Jack would also be instrumental in helping to fulfill this dream of a new life with his earnings from the sawmill. The two, father and son, worked at the mills for the next six years. Their dream was short-lived. On November 23, 1929, slightly more than six years after their arrival, Hubert Lee suffered from a tremendous headache. He died shortly afterward with what Jack said was diagnosed as a brain aneurysm. He was buried on the east side of the Black River in Concordia Parish, in a cemetery near the community of Wiseville, Louisiana. Hubert Lee Johnson was only fifty-three years old. His lifelong struggles and his dreams of a better life were now over.

———————

CHAPTER 20

IN DEAR AULD SCOTLAND, THE struggles continued. There was now a union with England and Scotland found itself under the rule of the English Kings. After the famine of the seventeen nineties, that claimed thousands of lives from starvation and disease, the Highlanders had found a crop that was suitable to their acidic lands. Potatoes had been planted after the Ireland Potato Famine in the eighteen forties.

The Blight that had devastated the potato crops in Ireland was discovered or thought to have had its inception in the United States where the potato blight had destroyed the potato crops there only a few years earlier. The Scots discovered that anywhere the depth of the soil permitted sufficient depth, the potato plant would grow and produce. That land was placed into production and the potatoes flourished. Production continued to expand until almost every small plot of land that had sufficient soil depth was producing the potato crop.

In the 1840s the potato blight that had hit Ireland now found its way to Scotland. Although not as severe and widespread as that of Ireland it still destroyed the crop that was now producing an economic boost to the Scots and providing a sustainable food supply. Crops were destroyed and the people again began to suffer from a shortage of food and employment. The people began to migrate to the larger cities in greater numbers.

As the migration to the cities and towns increased there now became a problem in housing and sanitation. It was reported that there was only one bathroom to care for the sanitary needs for each fifty plus individuals. Everywhere there was the smell and foul odor because of the unsanitary conditions. Housing or the lack thereof became another major issue in the larger populated areas. Because of the lack of adequate and sufficient housing for the influx of Scots, the landlords began to increase the rent to the point that all renters were feeling the burden of the higher cost of rent and the lack of adequate wages. Tens of thousands would leave Scotland bound for Australia, Canada and most would set their destination for the United States.

In the late nineteenth century steel was one of the major industries in Scotland. Summerlee Iron works and the Dalzell Iron Works of Motherwell, Scotland became the major employer of Scots. The company was owned by the wealthy Colville family. In 1872 the Dalzell Iron Works employed about 200 people. In 1879, John Colville, the owner of Dalzell, won the contract to supply and construct the Tay Bridge at Dundee, Scotland. This began the reputation of Dalzell which resulted in substantial growth and the winning of an even larger contract to construct the Forth River bridge in 1883.

A young man by the name of John Craig joined Dalzell as a thirteen-year-old teenager and trainee as an office boy. Craig's father was an employee of the Colville owned company, as a furnace man. In 1883 the company switched from Iron to steel and the future of the company was set. By the time the young Craig was twenty-one years old he had made an impression on the owners and an impact on the future of Dalzell Iron Works. He was promoted to represent the company in Glasgow at the Royal Exchange.

Although lacking in education, young Craig began studying and educating himself in his commutes between Motherwell and Glasgow. By the time, he was in his thirties he was well known and respected as a business man. At the age of forty-two he became Chairman of the company after the owners two sons died only months apart. From the time of his promotion to Chairman of the Colville Company, the company would grow and would soon employee 180,000 people.

During WW I, the Colville Company was the major supplier of shell casings and tank armor. Craig was now a well-known, respected and popular business tycoon. Colville was now at the top of steel production and John Craig was also at the very top. The rise to the top for Colville and John Craig would only last until shortly after the war. The Colville Company had already experienced a downturn in sales and production after WW I. By the early 1920s Colville would be forced to lay off tens of thousands of its workers.

Scotland had contributed greatly to the wars efforts and by the end of WW I the country had supplied over 700,000 of their best young men to the cause of the war. Of that 700,000 who gallantly served during the war, by November 11, 1918, they had lost nearly 120,000 killed in the fighting. After the war, Scotland men would have a difficult time finding employment for those returning from the war.

The company began to rebound because of shipbuilding and the demand for materials to support the war effort brought about by WW II. Colville would again be a major producer of shell casings, war armor and materials. During World War II, King George visited the company and made Craig Commander of the Order of the British Empire. The end of WW II would also present another downturn in steel production.

Neil Oliver noted in his book of the <u>History of Scotland</u>, two tragedies during and after the war which impacted those soldiers and their families. One was a train wreck near Dumfries-shires. The train carried almost five hundred soldiers returning from the front. The troop train collided with a coal train that was sitting stopped on the tracks due to a work crew's equipment that was on the wrong track. Only moments after the first crash another passenger train that was an express train, crashed head-on into the burning debris of the tangled steel and debris from the troop train and the coal train. The results of the crash were devastating in the death toll of the Scottish troops as well as the passenger train. Of the five hundred troops on the train there were 227 soldiers killed and 246 injured.

The second incident was a ship that had been placed into service because the ferry could not hold the large number of returning troops. Only yards from the Scottish shores near Stornoway, the ship whose captain was not familiar with the large cluster of rocks at the harbor mouth, crashed the ship into the rocks. The locals called the area "The Beasts of Holm". Almost all the troops aboard the ship could have told of the danger that the Beasts of Holm presented, had they known the Captain was not aware of the dangers below the surface of the frigid churning waters. There were now another 228-soldier's dead from drowning in the icy waters only yards from shore, a short distance from the harbor and in full view of the mothers, fathers, wives and children who watched in horror as their loved ones struggled to survive the icy waters.

When the war began and even before, the greedy landlords of the Scottish cities continued to exploit the cities struggling residents by raising the rent in every chance they could. During the war, they would evict the soldier's families who simply could not afford to pay the now ridiculous rental prices for the dilapidated shacks and apartments.

In 1916 there was an organized movement by tens of thousands of tenants to withhold the rent in protests. The government took notice and forced the Landlord's to reduce the rent back to the 1914 levels.

Between nineteen twenty through nineteen thirty, there were over half a million Scots who left Scotland. About fifteen percent of these simply crossed the border to England or went to Ireland.

Most of these again headed for Australia, Canada and most once again came to North America. These migrations of Scottish people to other parts of the world would calculate to twenty percent of all Scots, were now living in other parts of the world other than Scotland.

Shipbuilding became a part of the Scottish economy during the late seventeenth and early eighteenth century. In some respects, it was also tied to the tobacco crops that had become a tremendous part of the American economy. Some of the ships that were built were constructed for the explicit purpose of transporting goods to America and then returning to Scotland with a load of tobacco that went straight to the Scottish tobacco Lords and their now wealthy enterprise.

In many ways, the expansion of shipbuilding was a direct result of the expansion of the steel manufacturing in Scotland. During WW I the ship building necessity and its success was because the shipyards of Scotland only needed to be expanded to accommodate the now, necessary, large numbers of ships needed for the wars requirements. After the war, the Clyde shipyards suffered as much as the steel industry when the demand for ships and steel declined dramatically and threw the Scottish economy into a death spiral.

The real demand for the Scottish expertise of shipbuilding would again come during WW II. The shipyards of the Clyde met the requirements for this expansion. The Clyde opens out at Newark Castle at Glasgow and the Firth of Clyde and is where the great Scottish port of Glasgow is located. The port and shipyards continued to survive after the war until the demand for the great tankers were needed for transport of petroleum and other cargo.

It was at this turning point in the demands for larger vessels and especially the Super Tankers that the shipyards of the Clyde realized their dilemma. They simply could not build the super-tankers at the shipyard and then navigate the narrow water ways of the area. The mere size of these great ships could not be constructed within the shipbuilding walls and the Clyde shipyards went into decline. The Clyde shipbuilding that produced about thirty percent of the world's ships in 1950 went into decline and by 1960 they were only producing five percent of the world's ship building demands. The demands for more technologically advanced and larger vessels began to move to other parts of the world who could adapt and Scotland was to suffer the moving of these requirements to other shipyards.

The industries once crowded and backlogged order books had failed to realize the changes that were coming and they simply were not prepared for these changes. Unions also played big part in the declining state of Scotland's shipbuilding. They had jealously and zealously fought and protected the rights of specialty roles and trades of the workers and now found that this worked against them as these specialties were also becoming obsolete and needed to evolve with the industry which they had not expected nor had they prepared for.

—◆—

CHAPTER 21

THE NINETEEN TWENTIES WERE CALLED the Roaring Twenties. The ten years after World War I was considered a time of great wealth in the U.S. It was reported to be wealth in excess. The Johnsons in Louisiana were realizing a part of this success. Although their work was hard and the pay was only sufficient, they were determined to benefit from their hard work.

After his father's death, Jack, who was now seventeen, was on his own. He and his stepmother did not get along and Jack felt it best that he should move and begin life away from his stepmother. She later remarried and Jack lost all contact with her.

Jack would continue working at the mills but later moved into the home of a family named Sparks. The Sparks family were farmers who had a large farm on the Tensas River and east of Jonesville. Jack would also work on the farm and help with the chores.

Only a short time after his father died, disaster struck again. Not only for Jack Johnson but for people all over the world. In 1929, the Wall Street Crash of 1929 occurred. The Wall Street Crash, was also known as Black Tuesday. October 24, 1929 became one of the most devastating days in American History. The markets began to falter and fall and signaled a financial crisis that would stretch over the next ten years and become known as the "Great Depression". While building on post-World War I optimism, "that greatness was in the future for the economy of America", the people began migrating to the cities in large numbers with the hope of realizing a more prosperous life. The American industrial mechanism was at work and fortunes were abounding. Factories were expanding, manufacturing was at an all-time high and continued to flourish.

The American farmers were for the first time in their history realizing their dream. They had always worked hard with the hope that when their crop was harvested they could receive a fair price for their products. This had always been an important issue in the life of the farmer. He could not afford to plant more acreage because the prices for his product could take a down turn and it would prove disastrous. In the twenties things were changing. As factories continued to flourish the demand for farm products continued to grow all over the world and the prices soared. Many of the farmers could now plant more acreage and realize more profit. This resulted in even more acreage being planted to cash in on this growing demand.

While the American cities prospered, the overproduction of agricultural produce created widespread financial despair among American farmers throughout this ten-year period. With the overproduction, there was simply too much farm products to sustain the favorable prices. Now with the overproduction the demand began to falter and turn in reverse. The prices for grain and cotton began to decline and the farmers began to suffer. This would later be blamed as one of the key factors that led to the 1929 stock market crash.

The following is taken from public domain sources:

The Wall Street crash followed a speculative boom that had taken hold in the late 1920s. During the latter half of the 1920s, steel production, building construction, retail turnover, automobiles registered, even railway receipts advanced from record to record. The combined net profits of 536 manufacturing and trading companies showed an increase. In fact, in 1928 there was a record year, but for the first six months of 1929, there was an increase of 36.6% over 1928, itself a record half-year. Iron and steel led the way with doubled gains. Such figures set up a crescendo of stock-exchange speculation which had led hundreds of thousands of Americans to invest heavily in the stock market. A significant number of them were borrowing money to buy more stocks. By August 1929, brokers were routinely lending small investors more than two-thirds of the face value of the stocks they were buying. Over $8.5 billion was out on loan, more than the entire amount of currency circulating in the U.S. at the time.

When it was realized that at this record pace the American farmers would get more for their smaller crop than for that of 1928, up went stocks again and from far and wide orders came to buy shares for the profits to come in the near future.

In August, the wheat price fell when France and Italy were bragging of a magnificent harvest, and the situation in Australia improved. This sent a shiver through Wall Street and stock prices quickly dropped, but word of cheap stocks brought a fresh rush of "stags", amateur speculators and investors. Congress had also voted for a 100-million-dollar relief package for the farmers, hoping to stabilize wheat prices. By October though, the price had fallen to $1.31 per bushel.

Other important economic barometers were also slowing or even falling by mid-1929, including car sales, house sales, and steel production. The falling commodity and industrial production may have dented even American self-confidence. The stock market peaked just after Labor Day on September 3rd at 381.17, and then started to falter after well-known economics figure, Roger Babson, issued his prediction. The rising share prices encouraged more people to invest. People hoped the share prices would rise further. Speculation thus fueled further rises and created an economic bubble. Because of margin buying, investors stood to lose large sums of money if the market turned down-or even failed to

advance quickly enough. The average P/E (price to earnings) ra-
tio of S&P Composite stocks was 32.6 in September 1929, clearly
above historical norms.

Good harvests had built up a mass of 250 million bushels of
wheat to be "carried over" when 1929 opened. By May there was
also a winter-wheat crop of 560 million bushels ready for harvest in
the Mississippi Valley. This oversupply caused a drop-in wheat prices so heavy that the net incomes of the farming population from
wheat were threatened with extinction. Stock markets are always
sensitive to the future state of commodity markets, and the slump
in Wall Street predicted for May by Sir George Parish, arrived on
time. In June 1929, the prediction was saved by a severe drought in
the Dakotas and the Canadian West, plus unfavorable seed times
in Argentina and eastern Australia. The oversupply would now be
wanted to fill the big gaps in the 1929 world wheat production.
From 97¢ per bushel in May, the price of wheat rose to the $1.49
"market crash" forecast. By the end of September, the market was
down 10% from the peak (the "Babson Break"). Selling intensified in early and mid-October, with sharp down days punctuated
by a few up days. Panic selling on huge volume started the week
of October 21 and intensified and culminated on October 24, the
28th and especially the 29th ("Black Tuesday").

The president of the Chase National Bank said at the time:
"We are reaping the natural fruit of the orgy of speculation in
which millions of people have indulged. It was inevitable, because
of the tremendous increase in the number of stockholders in recent years, that the number of sellers would be greater than ever
when the boom ended and selling took the place of buying."

The Great Depression of 1929 was a worldwide depression that
lasted for ten years. Its kickoff in the U.S. economy was "Black
Thursday,". October 24, 1929. That's when 12.9 million shares of
stock were sold in one day. It was triple the usual amount. Over

the next four days, stock prices fell 23%. That was the stock market crash of 1929.

The height of the Depression was 1933. By then, unemployment had risen from 3% to 25% of the nation's workforce. Wages for those who still had jobs fell by 42%. Economic output, as measured by Gross Domestic Product, was cut in half, from $103 to $55 billion. That was partly because of deflation Prices fell 10% per year. Panicked government leaders passed the Smoot-Hawley tariffs to protect domestic industries and jobs. As a result, world trade plummeted 65% as measured in dollars and 25% in the total number of units. [Source: Public Domain]

The Depression caused many farmers to lose their farms. At the same time, years of erosion and a drought created the "Dust Bowl" in the Midwest, where no crops could grow. Thousands of these farmers and other unemployed workers looked for work in California. Many ended up living as homeless "hobos" or in shantytowns called "Hoovervilles," named after then-President Herbert Hoover.

As investors withdrew all their dollars from banks, the banks failed. That created more panic. The Feds ignored the banks' plight. This destroyed any remaining consumers' confidence in banks. Most people withdrew their cash and put it under their mattresses. This further decreased the money supply.

Thanks to the Feds, there was just not enough money in circulation to get the economy going again. Instead of pumping money into the economy, and increasing the money supply, the Feds allowed the money supply to fall by 30%.

In 1932, Franklin Roosevelt was elected President. He promised to create federal government programs to end the Great Depression. Within one hundred days, the New Deal was signed into law. It created forty-two new agencies designed to create jobs, allow unionization, and provide unemployment insurance. Many of these programs, such as Social Security, the Securities and Exchange Commission (SEC), and the Federal Deposit Insurance Corporation (FDIC) are still here today. They help safeguard the economy and prevent another depression. [2]

Many argue that World War II, not the New Deal, ended the Depression. However, if FDR could have spent as much on the New Deal as he did during the War, it would have ended the Depression. From 1932, when the New Deal was launched, until 1941, when Japan attacked Pearl Harbor, spending only increased the debt by $3 billion. In 1942, defense spending added $23 billion to the debt, and $64 billion in 1943. If that much had been spent on the New Deal, it would have been enough to end the Depression.

In fact, World War II had its roots in the Depression. Financial stress made people desperate enough to elect Hitler as Chancellor of Germany in 1933. He immediately began to consolidate his power through all means necessary. Even to the point of assassinating anyone who did not agree with him or anyone whom he perceived to be a threat. He quickly began to secretly rebuild the military, which was totally against the "Treaty of Versailles". We are very much aware of Hitler's attempt to murder the Jews in his death camps in Germany and Poland. If FDR and the U.S. had spent enough on the New Deal to end the Depression before Hitler consolidated his power, World War II might never have happened.

As everything was beginning to look good for the Johnsons for six years, the disaster that stretched all over the world tremendously affected those people living in the south and dependent on farms and the income from their production. Jack Johnson was caught in the middle of a fast falling economy. The earnings from the mills were gone as the mills closed because they could no longer sell their products, purchase timber and pay their employees. The farmer Jack was living with suffered greatly as the prices for

---

2 Roosevelt Institute, The New Deal.

his crops had plummeted and could now barely provide for his own family.

In 1930 Jack, could not find a job. All those living in the area around Jonesville struggled to feed their families. It seemed that everyone in the Jonesville area was suffering. Perhaps he could go to the larger city of Monroe and find work. Jack heard that work was plentiful in California. He first went to Monroe, Louisiana to again try to find work. Many people were now reduced to begging for food as they struggled to survive. When he arrived in Monroe he discovered that everyone in the larger city was no better off than the small town of Jonesville. In some cases, they were perhaps worse off. Employment was not to be found. Monroe's residents were struggling to find employment also. It seemed that the conversation and a solution to their problems turned to good news about California. People in central Louisiana were also hearing that work was plentiful in California. Now with no money, no job and without any prospects of finding work, he began to ask for assistance of anyone who could allow him to work and give him a meal. Working for a meal was common as the masses became even more desperate.

He finally made up his mind. He would leave the area of the country that he was familiar with and go to California. Maybe life would be better in California. Jack stated that he "hoboed" his way to California. He jumped on a train in Monroe that was headed west. He made it to Shreveport without being caught by the train detectives. He discovered that there were a large number of men trying to go west. Over the course of the next several weeks, Jack couldn't remember how long it took, he made it further and further west - through Dallas and Ft. Worth and the huge rail yards connecting rails leading in different directions and to various locals. He was determined to go west to find work and hid on a train heading west out of Ft. Worth.

He would on several occasions, find rest in various temporary camps that were always near the rails and near the towns. These camps were strung along the tracks at various places from Shreveport to California. They were always filled with men and occasionally with a man accompanied with his wife and sometimes a family with children. Everyone was experiencing the same situation. They were out of work, very little if any money and always the people were hungry. Yet they all had the same aspirations. Go where the work was and that was California. Many, if not all the men were content to try and find a meal any way they could. Some even resorted to theft if it meant they could have a meal. They were always on the lookout for a garden, a farm with an edible crop and always on the search for fruit orchards and Vineyards. They even scoured the area where there was a prospect for wild fruit.

Jack couldn't remember the exact course of his travels as he slowly made his way westward. He only knew that he desired to eventually end up in California and a wage-earning job.

So, he was relying on the trains and hoping their course was west to California. He would even take a job in the fruit orchards on his way to California, if any were available. But first he must reach California where the work was. Yet, as he traveled he realized there were more and more men with the same desire. They must reach California where the prospects of work were. They had heard now for months that there was plenty of work there for any man who was willing to work.

Along the way there was always the fear of being attacked for something so small as a piece of fruit. There was always the fear of assaults and robbery of their meager possessions. Most traveled with only the clothes they wore or with their meager belongings in a grass sack or flour sack. Then there was the ever-present danger of being caught by the railroad security and detectives. No one wanted to go to jail for trying to get a free ride on the train. They were all desperate to somehow survive the nation's worst disaster during their lifetimes. Many of the detectives would try to scare the men with threats but had no desire to have them arrested. Usually the ones arrested were the trouble makers. They knew the desperate situation these men and their families were in, yet they were required to do their job. After all that is what the railroad had hired them for, and they too were desperate to keep their jobs.

When Jack finally arrived in California, he quickly realized that people were there from various parts of the country. All with the same dilemma and desire, to find a job. There were farmers and their families who had traveled from various parts of the south. These were people who simply had lost their farms and had no other options but to find work where there was work. These work conditions or trying to find any available job in California would multiply when the Dust Bowl era hit in 1934 and 1936.

After searching for work over the course of several weeks and having to walk or hitchhike from place to place, Jack determined that there simply was no work. For any job that was available there were literally dozens or hundreds of men fighting for the same job. Always there were the same conditions that he had faced now for several months. There was no money, there was no food except what he could beg or some generous person would give him out of pity.

Realizing his plight, and facing the fact that the conditions were only expected to get worse, Jack decided to reverse his travels and head back to Louisiana. The situation could be no worse there. At least he would be in an area with which he was familiar. Over the course of the next several weeks he slowly made his way back to Louisiana. When he arrived back in Louisiana, he received updates on his family. He began to work on the farms doing odd jobs. He chopped cotton and when it was harvest time he picked cotton. It was not a good living and was hard work, but at least he was providing for himself.

—————◆—————

CHAPTER 22

AFTER HIS RETURN TO LOUISIANA, Jack discovered that his older half-brother William Lee Johnson was then back in Alabama. After their father, Hubert Lee had left them in Alabama to be raised by their mother, his older brothers had grown up and had lived an adventurous life. Hubert Canal Johnson had made his way to Vicksburg Mississippi before World War I, where he met and eventually married Ella Mae Riddle in 1913. The marriage lasted only a couple of years and they were divorced. When World War I began, Hubert Canal enlisted in the Army and went off to war. When he returned in 1917 he again made his way back to Vicksburg, Mississippi. After a short time in Vicksburg he traveled back to Alabama to the area where he was raised near Sipsey, Alabama and to be near his brother and his family.

His brother, William Lee, had married a lady from Birmingham, Alabama, named Annie Evert Hammons in 1909. They began their family there and had several children who were born in the Sipsey-Birmingham area. The brothers had been separated for a few years. Each brother had gone his separate way as Hubert Canal first had an unsuccessful marriage and then joined the army where he spent three years of his life. William Lee had even moved his family to Virginia for a short time where he began working in the coal mines. When Hubert Canal returned from the army and to the Vicksburg, Miss. area, around 1923. William Lee and his family returned to Mississippi where the brothers were reunited. The two brothers eventually moved to Brookhaven, Mississippi.

Family history records that the two brothers decided to go into business together in the late nineteen twenties. The problem with the business was that it was illegal. Their business venture was to set up a "whisky still" and make and sell "White Lightning" or "Moonshine Whisky". There was always a demand for Moon Shine even when the world's economy was in a decline. There was very little capital investment and the profits would be great. It would be a fool proof business venture. They simply couldn't lose. They needed to locate an obscure place in the woods and begin their business that would bring them the fortune they were dreaming of. They quickly discovered they were very wrong. The business didn't last long because the Federal Agents staked out their obscure and safe place. The agents caught the owners of the still and they served the next year in jail.

After their release from jail, the two brothers went to Bradford, Alabama where they both worked in the coal mines. Now the effects of the depression were having an effect on the entire nation. In 1931, William Lee and his family, along with Hubert Canal Johnson, moved to Tallulah, Louisiana for a short time. Jack had finally arrived back in Louisiana from his trek to California in search of work. He had found work in the cotton fields and was finally able to support himself.

The Depression was affecting everyone and any job that could be found was considered a blessing. The Depression was also affecting Hubert Canal Johnson and his brother, William Lee Johnson and his small family. They, too, were in search of work. One of William Lee's daughters had married and she and her husband had moved to Mississippi in search of work. They were also trying to follow the cotton harvest to earn a few dollars to survive. The cotton harvest was a sure thing for employment. Cotton prices were now somewhat stabilized and the cotton farmers were always desperate to get their crops harvested before the damp late fall weather made it impossible to harvest the cotton.

Beulah Alice Johnson had married Charles Robert Evans and now had two children. They had left the Bradford, Alabama area for Mississippi where the coal mines were now experiencing the financial crisis just as other industries were. They had heard that there was work in the cotton harvest and they were desperate to find work. When they arrived to the farm area of Mississippi they discovered that the harvest was complete. Charles told his wife that he would leave them there while he went in search of work. Beulah waited for her husband to return with good news of finding work to sustain the family.

William Lee received word from his brother Jack that there was a lot of work in the large cotton producing area of the Delta region of Louisiana and the cotton harvest was just getting underway. The family could probably earn enough money to carry them through the winter, with the entire family working in the harvest. William Lee and his family set out for Tallulah, Louisiana.

They knew that Beulah and her family were still in Mississippi. They decided to go by and see her and the children before proceeding to Tallulah. When they arrived, they discovered the dire straits that Beulah and her children were in. Her husband, Charles had left to look for work and had never returned. Rather than leave their desperate daughter and two children in Mississippi, they talked her into traveling to Louisiana with them. William was quoted as saying "ok, let's all go to Louisiana". They loaded her few belongings up and they all went to Tallulah, Louisiana and spent the fall picking cotton in the Louisiana Delta. Beulah never heard from her husband again. She nor her family would ever know what had happened to him. He had just disappeared. Since he was originally from Michigan, it was believed that he had deserted his wife and two children in Mississippi and had possibly gone back to Michigan.

After spending the fall in Louisiana, picking cotton, William heard from his son, Woodrow Wilson (Glen) Johnson. Woodrow had applied for a position with the C.C.C. corps and had been sent to North Carolina just prior to the family leaving Alabama for Louisiana. The **Civilian Conservation Corps** (CCC) was a public work relief program that operated from 1933 to 1942 in the United States for unemployed, unmarried men, from relief families as part of the New Deal. Originally it was intended for young men ages 18–23, but it was eventually expanded to young men ages 17–28.

When they heard from their son, the news was good. They were excited to learn that there was a lot of work and job opportunity in North Carolina. The entire family had been involved in the cotton harvest. The family now had some money saved from their hard work in cotton fields. William Lee and his family left for North Carolina. President F.D.R.'s "New Deal" efforts to save the country from the grips of the Depression were beginning to take effect and the results were positive.

William and his wife, Annie, and their children, along with Beulah and her children went to Greensboro, North Carolina. Beulah later remarried and she and her new husband would have a very large family over the years - including a set of triplets and two sets of twins! The entire families remained in North Carolina and their descendants remain in the Greensboro area today.

———————◆———————

CHAPTER 23

HUBERT CANAL HAD FOLLOWED HIS brother William Lee to the Tallulah, Louisiana area where his brother and his family were living before leaving for North Carolina. A young lady by the name of Annie Mary Edna Cole, traveled to visit her sister in Hot Springs, Arkansas after her marriage ended in divorce. She found employment and became a housekeeper in Hot Springs, Arkansas. She received news that another sister who was in Tallulah, Louisiana was having problems with her marriage and was having a very difficult time financially. Annie Cole quit her job and told her sister in Hot Springs that she was leaving for Louisiana to help their other sister.

When she arrived at her sister's home in Tallulah she discovered that her sister was indeed having a difficult time. She quickly realized that her sister's son, her nephew, had no shoes and few clothes that were wearable. She immediately took her savings from her housekeeping job in Hot Springs and bought new shoes and clothes for her nephew and her sister. When she finished, she had spent all her savings and now had no money for a bus ticket to return to Hot Springs. Rather than contact her sister in Hot Springs or her parents, for money for a return ticket, she had another plan. She went to the Company Store in the farming area and purchased a nine-foot cotton sack. She would pick cotton to earn enough money to buy her ticket and continue to help her sister and nephew who were in need.

Annie stated that when she went out to her job in the cotton harvest, she noticed a young man there who also needed a job picking cotton. The young man was Hubert Canal Johnson who had followed his brother William to Louisiana for the cotton harvest. Hubert Canal stated that "when I saw the young attractive and industrious Annie Marie Cole, I knew that I wanted a job picking cotton".

When the harvest was over, Annie now had enough money for her return ticket, however Hubert Canal, who was now very much infatuated by the young Annie, refused to allow her to buy the bus ticket and insisted that he drive her back to her home in Friendship, Arkansas, not far from Nashville. The two continued to keep in touch and they were married in March of 1939. Both Hubert and his brother William Lee had married ladies who were named Annie. The newly married couple returned to Tallulah, Louisiana where they decided to try their hand at farming. Hubert Canal had made some acquaintances in the Delta farming region, who were land owners. They sharecropped a farm in 1939-1940 but decided this was not the life they wanted.

The young couple decided to take their money and relocate back to Tennessee near Annie's parents. Their first son was born in Tennessee. In early 1943 Hubert and his wife Annie and their new son left for North Carolina where his brother William and his family were now living. William had written that work was plentiful in that area. They both began a career with the same company, which was Burlington Mills Manufacturing.

Hubert Canal "Pink" Johnson lived ninety-eight years and was listed as one of the oldest World War I veterans prior to his death in nineteen eighty-eight. He received a Certificate of Recognition from President Ronald Regan for his service in World War I. He was buried with Military Honors in Randolph County Memorial Park in Greensboro North Carolina and is noted as a World War I veteran.

Hubert Canal's brother, William Lee Johnson lived to be ninety-five years of age. He was born in July of 1889 and he died in 1984 in Greensboro, North Carolina, four years before his younger brother.

Another of Jack's brothers, the older brother, Roy Lee Johnson, heard that the two half-brothers were having success in North Carolina. William Lee had moved there in the late nineteen thirties and was followed by his brother Hubert Canal in 1943. Roy Lee now decided that he too would move to Greensboro, North Carolina. Roy Lee also found work at the same manufacturing plant as his two half-brothers. The three brothers worked for Burlington Mills Manufacturing Company. They had finally found their place of security and would spend the rest of their working careers, working for the same company. All three retired from Burlington Mills.

After Jack's return to Louisiana from his California venture he had remained in the Jonesville and Harrisonburg, Louisiana area. He was now known as Jack Johnson, and had now permanently changed his name from the name Zattie May, to Jack. After working the cotton harvests with his brothers, he returned to the Jonesville vicinity.

In 1933, Jack met an attractive young lady who lived in Harrisonburg, Louisiana. Katherine Cecil Husbands had lived all her life in the Harrisonburg area. Her mother's maiden name was Kelly. The Kelly family was a well-known family in the Harrisonburg, Catahoula Parish area. They had been in this area of Louisiana since the early 1800s and were the developers of the Kelly Plantation just outside the city limits of Harrisonburg. The plantation originally contained several thousand acres but had been subdivided over the generations to smaller farms. A Bayou named Kelly Bayou bounded the plantation on the west, The Harrisonburg hill country was to the north and Bersley Bayou to the south.

Katherine Cecil's father's name was Andrew Jackson Husbands. The Husband family could be traced back to 1610 in Portland, Dorset, England where they were known as Hosbandgh. Over the years and when they came to America they adopted the American spelling from Hosbandgh to Husbands. They would eventually migrate from Georgia to Louisiana and then to Catahoula Parish, Louisiana. In nineteen thirty-three, Jack was back in Harrisonburg, Louisiana. Harrisonburg, is only about fifteen miles from Jonesville and Jack had made several trips to Harrisonburg over the eleven years he had been in that area.

After courting for several months, the young couple decided to get married. Jack was now twenty-three years of age and Katherine was seventeen years of age. The couple set their wedding day and went to a nearby church to speak to the pastor and request that he marry them. The year is now nineteen thirty-four.

When the couple visited the well-known Pentecostal Preacher to request him to preside over the ceremony, the preacher first needed to confer with the young couple. As any good preacher who was faithful to his calling in the ministry would do, he asked them about their lives and what they desired for the future? Would they consider living a spiritual life and be involved in a church? In the conversation, the preacher had to fulfill his calling and ask if the young couple had accepted Jesus Christ as their Savior or if they desired to do so? Jack had been in a church very few times in his life and his future wife had been more often but still not a regular attender in the church-attending majority in this central Louisiana vicinity.

Both had to reply no to the first question and possibly to the second and third. The Preacher explained the benefits of a young couple beginning their marriage in regular church attendance and the joys of raising their future family while attending a church regularly. The couple was married a short time later in Katherine Cecil's older sister's home. The date was August 29, 1934.

A few months later after attending church at the Pentecostal Preacher's invitation, the young couple became Christians and began their church going attendance and involvement which would continue for their entire lives.

Jack had received only a second or third grade education before traveling to Louisiana with his father on the homemade barge. His formal education would end at that time as Jack began to work and not attend school. He also suffered what was later believed to be dyslexia. Dyslexia has various forms but one is where the letters or words appear as though one is seeing the words in reverse or as looking through a mirror. Although Jack could read some words, it took time for him to determine what the words were, which is a common trait for this learning problem.

Katherine Cecil would read to Jack and most of the time this reading was from the Bible, or as they studied their Sunday School lessons. Jack became what is known in the Christian circles and church denominations as "A Prayer Warrior". This is a person who believes and practices the benefits of a strong involvement in prayer. Jack and Katherine Cecil always prayed each morning prior to beginning their day. Many mornings the children would be awakened by their Mother and Father praying.

Each meal was only begun after a prayer of thanks was said. Each evening the father and mother would require that all the children kneel with them as they prayed before bedtime. Anyone who was visiting was always asked if they wanted to join the family in prayer. Jack always had a place of prayer that he would often go when he was home and that favorite place would usually be under a tree in the nearby woods. When Jack and Katherine Cecil decided to accept, the Pentecostal Preachers advise and raise their family in a Christian environment, they took it to heart and they never diverted from their mission.

Jack and Katherine Cecil would proudly state in later years that all their children had made a profession of faith and were attending church. Jack Johnson was never a preacher nor a Sunday School teacher but he had learned the teachings of the Bible and could quote Bible Verses as well as many church attenders who had an education. People who knew Jack's dedication to prayer would often seek him out to pray for them when they were ill or facing a problem in which they felt the situation required the spiritual involvement of prayer.

After Jack met Katherine Cecil in 1934 and they were married on August 29, 1934. Jack and Katherine Cecil moved to Harrisonburg Louisiana where their first son Andrew Hubert, was born on July 25, 1935. Jack began sharecropping and continued to farm until 1942. During this time, he had two other children born in the Catahoula Parish area. Elizabeth Maudell Johnson was born December 13, 1937 and Bobby Vernon Johnson was born December 28, 1940.

Jack decided to quit farming because of crop failures and when he heard that his brothers were in North Carolina and doing well he decided to go to Greensboro with his family. He quickly found work at Burlington Mills and the family continued to grow. Jack and Katherine's third son, Roy Lee Johnson was born in Greensboro North Carolina on November 27, 1943. He was named after his uncle who lived in Greensboro. After two years in North Carolina, Jack and his wife Katherine Cecil decided to return to the Louisiana.

Again, he began to try his luck at farming and bought a small farm near Enterprise, Louisiana, which was close to Harrisonburg, Louisiana. After other crop failures Jack was forced to give up on farming. He then began to work as a truck driver and hauled oil field equipment for a company that was headquartered in Harvey, Louisiana but had another company in Natchez, Mississippi.

Three other children were born to Jack and Katherine Cecil. A daughter, Ruth Evelyn was born on May 21, 1946, a daughter,

Patsy Christine was born September 15, 1947, and another daughter, Jackie Fay, was born June 27, 1956.

In 1947 the Johnson family was living in Ferriday, Louisiana. Jack and Cecil decided to take a trip to Harrisonburg, Louisiana to visit Katherine Cecil's mother. At that time, Jack, had bought a pick-up truck at a bargain price. The truck ran great but there was just one problem. Both doors had been wrecked and were removed and were to be replaced in the future but that time had never arrived. Although the repairs needed to be made, Jack continued to drive the truck with caution. The truck was to be used for the trip to visit Katherine Cecil's mother and was to take place early the next morning. The older four children were to ride in the back of the pickup with Katherine Cecil riding in the front with the two younger children. Patsy Christine was only a few months old and would be held by her mother.

When morning came, as was customary with Jack, he had to leave as early in the morning as possible. The entire trip was only about 50 miles, to Harrisonburg from Ferriday, Louisiana but the problem was, this was a trip where most of the roads in the area were still gravel, so the drive would be slow over the gravel roads and take longer. Jack wanted to be there as early as possible, visit and have lunch with Maude Husbands, Cecil's mother and then leave in the early afternoon so they could be home before dark. Everyone left Ferriday that morning with the older children in the back with blankets. The trip was going well and as the early mornings often were in this area of Louisiana there was some fog. As they were driving down the gravel road, in the country, a cow appeared in the road and was so close when Jack saw it that he had no way to stop or avoid hitting the cow.

Remember that the pickup had no doors and this was before seat belts. The only thing Jack could do was swerve to miss the cow. There was no time for warnings; he acted quickly and swerved to miss the cow. Katherine Cecil was holding the baby, Patsy Christine in her arms and they both went flying out of the pickup onto the gravel road. Desperately, Katherine Cecil's first instinct was to protect the baby. When Jack stopped the pickup, and expecting the worse, he ran back to check on his wife and baby. As he ran back he found Katherine Cecil holding the baby Patsy up, still in protective mode. Cecil had numerous gravel burns and bruises on her body with some cuts and scratches but no broken bones or injuries that required a visit to the doctor. The baby, Patsy Christine, only had a small scratch. Her mother had taken the brunt of the injuries to protect her baby daughter. The trip continued from there with a very sore Katherine Cecil, visiting her mother and having to explain how she had fallen out of the truck while holding her baby.

—————

CHAPTER 24

WHEN WORLD WAR II WAS just beginning, two of the Johnson brothers from the Arkansas birthplace joined the army. Hazel Johnson and Troy Johnson had been raised mostly by their half-sister and had remained in the Arkansas area. Both brothers served in the U.S. Army. After discharge from the army, both Hazel and Troy married but both marriages failed. In the future years both brothers became drifters. They would never settle down in any specific locale. Hazel would occasionally show up at his brother Roy Lee Johnson's home in North Carolina or at Jack's home in Louisiana. They would visit for a few days or a week and then leave again without any known destination

Troy Johnson was as equally a drifter as his brother Hazel. He remained in the central Louisiana area yet he never remained in one place for long. Troy and Hazel always knew where Jack was living and where their brother Roy Lee had always been in Greensboro. They always kept track of their brothers and when they needed assistance they would always show up or call.

We will now make a slight diversion from the narrative to relate the "Rest of the Story" as Paul Harvey would say.

The first time the Johnson children remembered seeing their Uncle Troy was in 1947 when they were living in Ferriday, Louisiana. Their Uncle Troy showed up one day and visited with the family and then as would be common over his life, he left again to roam the country as a drifter. The same was true for Hazel. After Troy visited Jack's family in Ferriday, Uncle Hazel also showed up a couple of months later for a few days' visit. Then as did Jack's brother Troy, Uncle Hazel left for parts unknown.

Hazel showed up in North Carolina in 1950 and visited his brother, Roy Lee and his half-brothers William Lee and Hubert Canal. He was told that Jack and his family were now in North Carolina and he paid Jack and his family a short visit. The family always took photos when the brothers visited because they did not know when or if they would ever see the drifters again. As was always the norm, he left and the brothers would only hear from him occasionally.

Hazel was reported to have died in 1976 in Detroit, Illinois. He was only sixty years old. The drinking and hard life took its toll on his health.

Sometime in late nineteen seventy-seven Jack went to Monroe. He had not heard from his brother Troy for several years. Jack decided to try and trace down his brother Troy. Troy was known to visit Monroe frequently over the years. Jack began talking with a man in Monroe who was also a drifter and discovered that he and Troy were acquainted and were friends, however he did not know where Troy was at the time. Jack gave the man a message to deliver to his brother Troy, when he next saw him. The message was that his brother wanted to see him and Jack left his address in Clayton, Louisiana.

A short time later a man with a long white beard and long silver hair appeared in Clayton to visit Jack and his wife. It was his brother Troy. The friend had delivered the message and Troy was responding to his brother Jack's request. Troy stayed for several weeks with Jack and Katherine Cecil. This would be the longest visit that Jack had ever known his brother to have with any member of his family. He didn't drink during his entire visit which was a big change for Troy. During his stay, he shaved off his white beard and

Jack paid for his brother to get a haircut. Troy would join Jack and Katherine Cecil in their nightly prayer time.

Bobby visited his father and mother for a couple of days and discovered that his Uncle Troy was there. This was the first time that he had seen his Uncle Troy in many years. It was discovered that Troy was very ill. He was bleeding and it was believed that he had colon cancer. When Bobby was ready to return to Lubbock, Texas where he worked, Uncle Troy decided it was time for him to leave also. With no home and no destination in mind he wanted Bobby to take him to Natchez, Mississippi. He said goodbye to Jack and Katherine Cecil and he and Bobby left for Natchez. He wouldn't tell anyone where he was going and said he was not sure. Bobby gave his Uncle Troy some money and Uncle Troy assured Bobby that he would not spend the money for drinking. His said his drinking days were over and his life was changed. Apparently, Jack and Katherine Cecil's Christian lifestyle had made an impact on him. They said goodbye. And this was the last time anyone ever saw Troy.

In 1978, a message was received from authorities in Monroe, Louisiana. The message was that Troy Johnson had died. He had in his possession the name and address of his beloved brother Jack and they needed Jack to come to Monroe to claim the body. Jack drove to Monroe and identified and claimed the body of his drifter brother. Jack arranged a funeral for his brother and Troy Johnson was buried in Delta cemetery, LaSalle Parish, Jena, Louisiana. He had apparently died of colon cancer at the age of seventy.

CHAPTER 25

———◆———

SHORTLY AFTER THE INCIDENT OF Katherine Cecil being ejected from the pick-up truck with no doors, Jack left his job with the oilfield company and tried farming again. The year was now 1949 and the family had moved across the Ouachita River from Enterprise, Louisiana. The main crop was cotton and the spring planting was begun when the heavy rains from north Louisiana and southern Arkansas and also in the Enterprise area caused the rivers to begin to rise. No one expected the outcome.

The rains continued and the river continued to rise. About two miles south of the farm was the junction of another river that flowed from east of Monroe, Louisiana and joined the Ouachita River a few miles south of Enterprise and between Harrisonburg and Enterprise. This river was the Boeuf River. It was not uncommon in this area for the floods up north to wreak havoc on the lower lying farms and forests down river. Normally, within a few days the water would recede with very little or no damage. This year was different.

The rains continued up north and in the area where the Johnsons lived. Flood warnings went out as the rivers continued to rise and before long they were over their banks all along the Ouachita and the Boeuf Rivers. The land between the Boeuf and Ouachita Rivers were slowly covered with the murky waters from their intersection and miles back toward the north and east in all the lower terrain. There was very little time for any of the families in the low-lying farm land to prepare for the fast-rising water. Within a few days all the newly planted crops were destroyed. All the labor and expense of preparing the land and for planting would now need to be repeated if the flood waters receded in time. This was an unexpected expense for the struggling farmers, which they could not afford.

The Red Cross began to come into the area to assist the flooded families. The state and federal government began to send assistance to provide much needed supplies to the flood victims. Most had no other place to go except the hill country on the Enterprise side of the river. As the rain continued and the waters continued to rise the main highway from Enterprise to Harrisonburg was also under water. Now the only open routes were the narrow gravel roads through the pine hill country to LaSalle Parish and Jena.

When the water leveled off, it was about two feet deep in the Johnsons home, which was already constructed on pier and beams and was about three feet above the ground. The flood waters eventually covered thousands of acres between Monroe, Columbia, Harrisonburg and Jonesville, Louisiana. The floods were comparable to the floods of 1929 which were on record as one of the worse the area had known to date.

The Red Cross provided tents for some of the families who had no place to live until they could return to their homes. A large military size tent was provided for the victims and the Johnson family was one of the recipients. A neighbor that lived about one mile down the river was Katherine Cecil's niece and her husband. The young couple owned a family farm which was one of the highest areas of land on the east side of the river. The floods had destroyed much of their newly planted crops but their home and several acres were still not affected. Since much of their farm was still high and dry, they allowed the Johnson family to set up the tent on their property.in a small clearing. A boat was used to deliver the tent and some supplies to the place where the tent would be set up.

To the Johnson children this was just another adventure. Bobby, Roy and Hubert would paddle the boat through the flooded woods or forest to their flooded home almost on a daily basis. There was no problem paddling through the flood waters because they would follow the gravel roadway from one location to the other and away from the treacherous currents of the river. Most of the items that were not needed to survive while living in the tent had been raised above the water level in the home. If their mother needed something, then the boys would paddle through the floodwaters to their home to retrieve the needed item.

One way to make the paddling trip shorter was to take a straight line through the flooded woods and what locals called "the back water". This way they could take a more direct route to their flooded home. On one such excursion, Bobby who was eight or nine and Roy who was six were sent on a mission for their mother. Bobby could swim but Roy had not yet learned to swim. Life jackets were not even considered as a means of safety for most of the population living on or near the rivers. Both boys were usually involved in paddling. Roy would always sit on the seat nearest the front of the boat and Bobby would occupy the back seat. The person in the back was responsible for guiding the boat and dodging the trees and debris in the floodwater. Bobby failed at his duty to steer the boat and the front of the boat hit a large tree. The impact caused Roy to lose his seating and he went flying out of the boat.

Remember, he was unable to swim. Bobby, realizing the emergency, jumped out of the boat and into the flood waters to help his younger brother. The water was deep enough that it was over both boys' heads. Bobby didn't have time to think but reacted quickly, not realizing that the force of his jumping would automatically propel the boat farther away from both of them. When he reached his brother, he realized that now another emergency and crisis had just been created. He grabbed his brother and tried to hold him up but the water was over his head. The boat was now several feet away and continued to drift even farther. There was only one option. Bobby would hold his brother and placing his feet on the ground below jump towards the boat. As he rose above the water he would take a breath of fresh air and again jump. After several jumps in this manner the two boys finally reached the boat. Now exhausted, they struggled to get back into the boat.

From that time on, they were more careful but this did not deter their boat excursions which would take them on many adventures during their teen years. Bobby would later joke that he should receive partial credit for Roy's success in life because, after all, he had saved his little brother's life in the flood of 1949.

When the floodwaters went down there was still time to plant the spring crops and Jack was able to plant his fields. He had lots of worries as he considered his failures at farming in the past. He had just experienced the additional expense of replanting the flooded and lost crop. With the spring flood of 1949 he was now very worried that he was facing still another failure at farming. There were just too many variables that could lead to disaster and failure. This was just one of them. The weather was always of major concern: too much rain, not enough rain, insects or other problems could occur. The flood was only a reminder of the disasters that could take place of which the farmer had no control.

As the new crop seeds began to sprout and grow Jack received news from his brothers in Greensboro, North Carolina. They had heard from Katherine Cecil that the floods had destroyed and would possibly prevent the planting of this year's crop. Jack's brothers wrote him that Burlington Mills was hiring and that Jack could probably go to work. He had worked there in 1942-1944, before he and his wife became homesick to see Katherine Cecil's aging mother and her siblings and returned to Louisiana.

Katherine's mother had died that same year in 1949, in Harrisonburg not too many months after the accident which resulted in Katherine Cecil and baby Patsy falling out of the truck.

CHAPTER 26

———————————

JACK CONSIDERED THE MOVE TO North Carolina again and discussed the options with his wife. The crop was planted and was growing. He couldn't just up and leave everything. He was committed. However, there was one option available. Maybe one of the nearby farmers would be interested in buying his new crop. Sure, enough there were some farmers with whom he talked who were interested. The deal was made and Jack received enough cash to purchase a pickup and had enough money remaining to make the trip to North Carolina. They would have enough money to find a home there and Jack would go to work at Burlington Mills.

The Johnson family loaded all their possessions onto the pickup truck and a small trailer. The problem was organizing the household belongings so that the now six children and the wife could make the trip. So, the most unique loading plan was devised. The first thing to be loaded in the pickup bed would be a mattress for the older children to sit and lay on. Then the other belongings would have to be arranged in such a way that the children in the back could be protected from the weather. Also, to be considered was where to spend the nights. Motels were not an option. There simply was not enough money for the family of eight to stay at hotels and eat in restaurants. They would need to conserve every dollar they could for their arrival in North Carolina and rent a home for the family.

So, the remaining mattresses and tarp would need to be arranged in such a manner that they could be removed at night so the family could set up camp near the roadside for the nights and then placed back on the truck for travel the next day. Travel would be slow, considering pulling the trailer, the load of household items and the large family. The remaining mattresses and bed frame items were arranged so as to give stability on the side of the pickup bed. They were placed on the side of the pickup bed standing on edge leaving a "cave" between the mattresses and few sturdy bed pieces for the children to be safe. At least four of the older children would ride in the back with Jack's wife, Katherine Cecil and the two younger girls riding in the cab.

Jack and Katherine Cecil had been very religious almost all their married life. From their early involvement in church, they were totally committed and this included a commitment to prayer. So, Jack and Katherine Cecil's children were also involved in the church. Prayer was a must for Jack and his wife. He always designated a time in the early morning and in the evening, before going to bed for a special time set-aside for prayer. He could often be heard in the woods near their home, praying. But these were not the only times for prayer. Jack would pray when he felt the need. Perhaps it was the utterance of a simple praise or a prayer for something and someone who had requested that he pray for them. Every meal was begun first with a prayer of thanks.

As the old pickup truck and trailer were loaded down for the long trip to North Carolina there was a lot of praying taking place. There is one family photo of the family as they were loaded and ready for this next adventure. The family members are standing beside the loaded down pick-up and trailer and one wonders how it could have all happened. But the trip was on and there was no turning back

The travel would take them through Natchez, Mississippi then east toward Birmingham and Atlanta, then to Greensboro, North

Carolina. Keep in mind that there were no interstates at that time and the roads of travel were much different than they are today. There were state highways and also U.S. designated highways that would take you through several states. There would be several stops through the day. Always there would be a scream for a restroom stop that usually took place in the trees beside the road. Then there were the stops for eating. There was always enough bread and baloney or lunchmeat for sandwiches during the day. The big issue was the stops for the evenings and nights. There was no driving that would take place at night. The Johnson family would always stop. Jack and his wife would look for a good place that was right to set up camp for the night and they would pull in. The mattresses and tarp would be removed and the tarp stretched out for cover for the night.

The evening meals were almost always sandwiches but occasionally there would be prepared food that was easy to prepare. Jack always had to have his coffee, so there would be a small fire to boil the water and make the coffee. The children had the responsibility of gathering a few sticks of broken limbs from trees so the fire could be started. This became a game for the children as their adventure grew with each mile of travel.

The stops along the roadside were always a time for their travel adventures to be even more special as they explored the new parts of the world. One such evening placed them beside the road near a large cornfield. It was now late spring and the corn was at the perfect maturity for corn on the cob. They were sure the farmer wouldn't care or perhaps and almost certainly Jack first asked but all the Johnson family enjoyed corn on the cob that night.

The travel was good and the newly purchased old truck did its job as it pulled the trailer and its heavy load through Mississippi and Alabama. Jack would gently nurse the truck up one hill or mountain and gently coast down the other side. When they were somewhere in the mountains of Georgia, a near disaster occurred.

As they were going down one mountainside Jack suddenly heard a noise and felt something break. He had suddenly lost control of the steering. Thankful that he wasn't going very fast he nursed the truck and trailer to the side of the road. As he checked the front end and the steering parts he discovered that one of the tie rods on the old truck had broken. The tie rod connects to the ball joints that hold the wheels into position. The family had been lucky that Jack was not driving fast and that he was able to get the truck stopped without further damage.

Now there was another problem that needed to be addressed. How was he going to make the repairs so the family could continue the trip? More prayers! The family had passed through a town several miles earlier so Jack had no other options. He not only had to hitchhike back to the town but then find the correct part and someone to help him make the repairs. The family would wait anxiously for him to return and know what the progress was or if he was successful. After several hours, a pickup truck pulled up and Jack got out.

Jack had found a wrecking yard in the town and somehow found the very part that was needed to replace the broken part. But that's not the end of the story. The driver of the other pickup was a mechanic from the wrecking yard who brought his tools and began to work on the family truck. He successfully replaced the part and the Johnson family was ready to begin their journey again. When Jack tried to pay the mechanic, he refused to allow Jack to pay him. Perhaps he saw the truck and trailer with six children running around and decided it was better to be generous and refuse payment. Either way Jack's prayers were answered again.

When they arrived in North Carolina they made their way over to Jack's brother, Roy Lee's home. The family stayed there for a few days while searching for a home to rent and for Jack to apply for a job at Burlington Mills. He received the job and found an apartment that was connected to the apartment owner's home. The family rented that apartment for a few months until another home was located closer to Jack's place of employment.

The apartment was owned by an elderly lady. As were many homes in this area in the nineteen fifties, the source of heating and cooking was from coal. When coal is burned it not only creates black smoke but also leaves a sooty and oily residue. After a prolonged usage, the soot accumulates on the ceilings. The elderly lady had a sooty ceiling in her home that needed cleaning. She now had two young boys, Hubert and Bobby, who could help her in the cleaning project.

She made an unusual purchase to clean the soot from the ceilings. She purchased some large rectangular bars, larger than a bar of soap but had the texture and looked similar to oversized gummy erasers. When they were rubbed across the ceiling they removed the soot in the same manner that an eraser would remove a pencil mark. After several days of hard work the elderly lady's ceilings were as clean as two young boys could make them. The pay to the two boys was not substantial in the way of cash but surely, she had made an agreement that she would reduce the rent as partial payment for the strenuous cleaning job.

After a short time, Jack found a home for rent near the plant where he was employed. This home was also near a large tobacco warehouse where the tobacco growers brought their tobacco after it was cured out. The farmers would gather at the warehouse each weekend after the tobacco was harvested and cured and their tobacco would be auctioned and sold to the large tobacco companies. The older boys would always try to go to the tobacco warehouse when there was an auction. The drawing card was not the tobacco but the free hot dogs and soft drinks that were provided for the farmers and their children. Who would know that these boys were not part of one of the farmer's family? What a great picnic and just another adventure in the lives of the Johnson children.

CHAPTER 27

———◆———

THE JOHNSONS LIVED IN GREENSBORO for almost two years when again they would return to Louisiana. Jack would reveal to his children in later years that it was a great mistake for him to leave his job at Burlington Mills. The reason for his leaving was explained. A higher position had become available and Jack felt that he should get the promotion. It was instead given to a less deserving individual and Jack quit his job. The old saying goes like this "cut off your nose to spite your face".

Jack now began to work for the oilfield company where he had worked several years earlier. It wasn't long before the company closed their truck yard in Natchez, Mississippi. Jack was given the opportunity to go to the company headquarters in Harvey, Louisiana, which he accepted. The immediate problem was that he would have to wait to take his family. They would remain in Harrisonburg until he could afford to rent another home and move his family to south Louisiana.

There was a home available on a portion of Katherine Cecil's old ancestral home place on what at one time was the Kelly Plantation. The Johnson family moved in and a short time later Katherine's sister and her family moved to another home nearby. Katherine's brother in law had just been hired on a bridge project that would replace an old bridge on the main highway between Jonesville and Harrisonburg, Louisiana. The project would take over a year and Jack continued to work in Harvey and return when he could. The family was comfortable and near other family members, so everything was fine.

When the bridge project was completed Katherine's sister and her family returned to Jena, Louisiana where they had a home in an area of Jena named Milltown. This was not a name of an incorporated town but only a name that the area became known as. The name was appropriate because an entire community had been built around two sawmills that operated there. Katherine did not want to remain on the old plantation home because it was far removed from easy access to Harrisonburg. Another home was available in Jena near her sister and her family so the Johnsons rented the home and Jack continued to work across the Mississippi River from New Orleans in Harvey, Louisiana.

Shortly afterward, Bobby became very ill with kidney albumin and was hospitalized for over two weeks as he struggled to recover. When he was released from the hospital, Jack found a home for rent between Harvey, Louisiana and Belle Chasse, Louisiana. The home was not far from the U.S. Naval Base in Belle Chasse, which a few years later would expand and take in all of the area where the Johnsons had lived. After they were living in Belle Chase for several months Katherine Cecil's sister, Alva contacted the family.

Alva is the sister whose husband worked on the construction of the bridge near Harrisonburg. The sister informed Katherine Cecil that her husband was having a difficult time finding a good paying job in the Jena area. Jack talked to the company he was working for to see if there was a possibility of him going to work there at Tom Hicks Transfer Company. The company hired him and the family came to live with the Johnson family until they could get settled. After working in Belle Chasse for a couple of months, tragedy struck.

Jack came rushing in with some bad news. Katherine Cecil's brother in law had been killed in an accident. A company crew, that included Jack and his brother in law, had a piece of equipment that was called a turntable for a pile driver. The equipment was on one tractor trailer that they were preparing to unload from one eighteen-wheeler trailer rig and place it on another trailer for transport. Apparently, a mechanical problem had developed on the trailer that it was currently loaded on. They had backed one eighteen-wheeler trailer close to the other with only a close space between the two trailers. As they were preparing the rigging for the change Jack's brother in law walked between the trailers to adjust a piece of the rigging. Something caused some movement and the pile driver turntable began to move. When the crew yelled to the brother in law to warn him of what was taking place he turned to see what the problem was. By that time the Turntable was at the edge of the trailer and he couldn't move to a safe place to get out of the way of the sliding piece of heavy equipment. He was crushed to death between the two trailers. After the funeral, Katherine's sister and her children moved back to Jena, Louisiana to their family home and remained there until her children graduated from high school

In the years that followed, the Johnsons eventually moved back near Jonesville, Louisiana. Jack Johnson continued to work in South Louisiana until he had a medical scare that would limit his work for several years. He had developed a heart condition that required complete rest for a lengthy period of time. Arrangements were made to travel to New Orleans to pick Jack up and bring his car and belongings back to the Jonesville area. Alva, Katherine Cecil's sister, used her car and an uncle went with them to drive Jack's car. Bobby went along because he could remember the route they needed to travel and the places to turn so he would ride back with his uncle. There were several tricky turns and road changes at Baton Rouge that would take them though Natchez, Mississippi and Bobby knew these road changes.

This became a trying time for the Johnson family as they tried to survive with the reduced income. Because of the reduced income, the Johnson family received government assistance which included a program called "Commodities". This was a program set up for needy families where they would, once each month, receive a various assortment of food supplies. These supplies included flour, corn meal, powdered milk, canned meat, beans, rice, shortening, peanut butter and cheese. To say the least, this was a time of humility but a time where the Johnsons were very appreciative of assistance. The children looked forward to the day the Commodities were received because the cheese and peanut butter were considered a special treat.

When Bobby and Roy were only around ten years of age and their father was working in south Louisiana, the young boys became skilled hunters. They had a one shot twenty-two rifle that they used often for hunting rabbits. In the fall and winter, they would hunt several nights each week. Their hunting was not for sport but for survival. Usually their hunting skills meant that the family would have meat on the table for their next meals.

They had acquired a battery-operated headlight to go along with their one-shot rifle. During the fifties, the "carbide light" was used often as a useful night light for hunting or for night fishing. The "carbide light" used carbide pellets and when mixed with water produced a gas that was flammable. The shield around the burning gas nozzle was reflective and the flame could be adjusted to produce the most effective beam. A special head gear was needed to mount the carbide light. There were clips or hooks to hold the light to the headgear and this type of light also had its dangers since the gas was explosive. Although the brothers were experienced in using this type of light, the battery-operated head light was the most effective and easier to use.

The brothers would make their nightly hunting excursions through the "old Kelly plantation" skirting the wooded areas around the pasture or fields for rabbits or an occasional raccoon. The rabbits could be easily detected because when the light was on them, their eyes would reflect a brilliant color as the headlight spotted them. The boys would carry an old grass sack or flour sack to place their game after a successful shot.

The ammunition was never used for pleasure shots. To them each bullet was an important and treasured object that was carefully protected. They very seldom had the money to buy an entire box of twenty-two cartridges. They could only acquire enough change to purchase about ten bullets. Bobby and Roy became skilled hunters. They very seldom required more than one shot to kill their game.

When they made their nightly kill, they would return home and dress and clean their next day's meal. Their mother had taught them to always place the fresh, wild game in a pan of salty water or water with vinegar to remove any wild game taste. Their mother would then take the game and use a special batter for frying the next day, making another delicious meal for the family. Their hunting skills carried them through their early teen-age years.

The Johnson children usually worked to help the family. At the age of ten and eleven Hubert and Bobby were in the fields with their parents chopping or picking cotton to earn money for the family. When Jack was out of a regular job, the older children were always needed in the fields in the spring and summer. It was necessary for the family's survival.

They were also involved in "Chopping Cotton" in the spring. This effort was a necessary part of farming and was just as demanding as picking cotton. All farms and crops need the grass and weeds removed so the newly sprouting and growing crops can flourish. If a crop was not properly cared for by the removal of the weeds and grass, then the crop production would suffer accordingly. This was not something that only occurred once during the spring and summer but sometimes it would require this cleaning process called chopping, several times during the growing season.

The farmer would cultivate the crop to eliminate the weeds and grass between the rows. He could not get the cultivators close to the root system without damaging the crop. After he cultivated the crop the family and/or the hired workers would take sharp hoes and complete the cleaning of the weeds and grass near the row of young plants. This was the time that the planted crop was also thinned. Too many of the cotton or corn plants would also reduce the yield. As the laborers chopped the grass and weeds they would thin the plants, usually the width of the hoe. They would leave two or three of the cotton or corn plants, then they would remove one hoe width of grass and weeds and then leave two or three more plants. This cycle was repeated through the entire field. The first chopping was always the most critical because this was the time to thin and remove any plant that would use the nutrients that were needed for the crop. The next time the crop was chopped only the grass and weeds were removed. As the crop plants grew larger they then shaded out the grass and weeds and became a natural process of reducing the growth of the unwanted grass and weeds.

The Johnson children were often involved in picking cotton as were most children living on the farms, even when they were not farming. They would often hire out to farmers near their home who were in need of additional hands to pick the cotton. All cotton picking was done by hand. There was a long sack usually six to nine feet long. The length of the sack usually depended on how strong you were or how fast you could pick cotton. There were also smaller sacks for the smaller children because children of all ages were involved in the cotton harvest.

The weather was always a factor. The pickers began picking when the dew from the night had dried from the cotton and

continued picking until sundown. Some of the better cotton pickers would take two rows at a time. These were usually the men or
women who could pick three hundred plus pounds of cotton per
day. Some of the better pickers would often team up with someone
else and they would take three rows between them. Each would
share the third row. The burrs around the cotton were sharp and
often they were picking with sore or even bloody fingers. You had
to pull the locks from the bowls to reduce any unwanted material. Any debris in the cotton would result in a lower grade at the
gin because the higher quality or grade of the cotton meant more
money for the farmer.

When the sacks were full, the picker would have to carry their
sack to the cotton trailer where it was weighed, recorded and emp-
tied and they would return to fill their sack again or pick until
sundown when they would make the final weighing and empty
the sacks. Usually a bale of freshly harvested cotton would require
about fifteen hundred pounds to be ginned. The ginned bale
would be reduced to about five hundred pounds after the seeds
had been removed.

Most of the experienced cotton pickers could pick between
three hundred and even four hundred pound per day. Most of
the teenagers could pick about one hundred fifty pounds per day.
Considering that most farmers paid around four dollars per hundred, maximum, one can understand why this was usually a family
effort. Even with a family of four the family could only earn about
thirty dollars per day. When the families saved, they could barely
save enough to manage through the winter, or until spring cotton
was planted and the chopping season would begin.

C H A P T E R   2 8

———

BOBBY, HUBERT, AND THEIR MOTHER Katherine would find jobs of chopping cotton during the spring and summer. They were living on a farm that was owned by the pastor of a church they attended. His name was Preacher Wiley. There were other farms on the side of the river where they lived but these were over a mile away. Jack drove the car around to their home, which was about a thirty or more-mile trip from Jonesville, through Ferriday and Clayton, Louisiana then gravel roads back toward their home with the last mile or two miles, being dirt. The narrow dirt road leading to their home was often muddy after a rain and care was taken not to bury the car up in the mud. They then had transportation to the neighboring farms where they would travel to chop cotton.

Preacher Wiley had a barge he used for his tractor and trailer but it was not possible to get a car off and onto the barge and drive up the steep riverbank. When they were working Elizabeth Maudell, who was the oldest daughter and second child of Jack and Katherine Cecil, would always take care of the younger children and the household chores.

Andrew Hubert was the oldest son of Jack and Katherine Cecil. Hubert was always obtaining books and magazines from any source possible. Jack would not allow the children to read comic books but somehow Hubert would obtain these comic books and eventually they would be added to his treasured collection of books and magazines. He would read and study the magazines and would not allow any of his siblings to touch his treasures which would continue to pile up in his private hoard. He joined the navy in 1955 and spent the next four years traveling the world and the seas of the world.

Preacher Wiley would hire Bobby for work that was needed and Bobby worked alongside the preacher's son who was also a close friend. They were near the same age of fourteen. One of the jobs was cutting timber. The preacher was clearing some additional property for farming so they would cut the logs to be hauled to the sawmill. This became quite an ordeal for the young teenagers and the preacher. The farm was isolated across the Tensas River from other active farms and homes. There were no homes within one mile of the preacher's farm and could only be reached by a narrow dirt road on that side of the river. The easiest access was from the main highway going from Jonesville to Ferriday. There was a gravel road near the levee directly across the river from Preacher Wiley's farm. This made access to Jonesville only a few miles. But the family had to leave the car on one side of the river and cross the river by boat.

The Tensas River was narrow at this point and the Preachers barge was only large enough for his tractor and equipment. The Tensas River was narrow at this point. Preacher Wiley had connected a large rope from one bank of the river to the other and used small pieces of steel for anchors to hold the rope down. The rope was used to pull the barge from one side of the river to the other. He had made an entrance and egress road going down to the barge. The banks of the river were always muddy and soft from the silt that built up. Although the barge had some ramps, they were often not long enough to reach the dryer bank, especially when there was a load on the trailer that needed to be taken across.

When they cut the logs, they would load them on a trailer for transport to the sawmill, which was in a community on the main highway between Jonesville and Ferriday. Loading the logs was an ordeal of mostly manual labor. The logs would be pulled by a small Ford tractor, over to a small cleared area to be loaded on the trailer. Two poles would be placed on one side of the trailer and the small tractor that was used quite extensively on the farm and the land clearing was set up on the other side. Chains would be tied to the tractor and stretched across the trailer and attached to the log. With the use of the tractor and two fourteen-year-old teenagers pushing and controlling the log it was slowly skidded up the poles and onto the trailer. When the trailer had all the logs and weight that could be handled by the trailer they headed for the barge at the riverbank. Now another ordeal would begin.

Although there were several long boards used to keep the trailer from slipping off and becoming stuck, this very thing would happen quite often. The greatest difficulty would almost always be on the other side of the river where exiting the barge began. The Preacher would rev up the tractor for the exit and the climb up the bank but often as the trailer hit the boards that had been laid as an exit ramp, the wheels of the trailer would slip off and no amount of pushing, pulling or discussing the situation would solve the problem. (No cussing would help nor was it allowed) The two teenagers would always think to themselves, "well he has done it again".

Now the logs or several of them would have to be unloaded to lighten the load. The wheels that were buried in the mud would have to be jacked up, shovels used to level the muddy tracks, the boards replaced under the wheels and the preacher would again take his position as the tractor driver and make ready for the final run up the river bank. He would again rev the tractor and take off with the tractor wheels spinning and two teenage boys pushing with all their strength, to the top of the riverbank where the pickup was awaiting to complete the journey to the sawmill. The unloaded logs would have to be pulled up the hill with the tractor and then reloaded on the trailer for the final part of the arduous journey which was completed with the trailer being towed by the pickup.

There was one consolation to all the strenuous work that was required when they were clearing the land or other farming choirs with Preacher Wiley. He always brought sandwiches for lunch but the other part of the meal was the treat that they always looked forward to. Preacher Wiley always allowed the two teenagers to get an RC cola or a NEHI drink with a small cake as part of their lunch. This was usually a moon pie or a small cake that was shaped like a half moon but had fruit and nuts in it. These were similar to a fruitcake but they did not have as much fruit and nuts in them. This was considered a great treat because it was rare, except on these working occasions to have a soft drink, although they were only ten cents and the cakes were about five cents. Most of our money was used to support the family at this time and after a hard week's work, we would on the weekend, have enough money to indulge in one of the soft drinks and perhaps an ice-cream cone at the Jonesville Pharmacy and fountain bar.

It was on one of these Saturday gatherings at the local fountain bar that one of Preacher Wiley's younger daughters was in the street and was run over by a car, literally run over. When she was hit by the car and knocked to the pavement the car ran completely over her and she was not hit by the wheels. Somehow, she survived with only minor bruises.

When several months later, all the logs were finally cut and hauled to the mill there began another adventure that was very unusual for two teenage boys who were now around fourteen or fifteen years of age. It was then necessary to pile the limbs and debris from the logging operation and burn the piles. Again, the little Ford tractor was the workhorse along with the strong backs of the two teenagers. The real adventure was now about to commence. The use of dynamite? Yes, Dynamite! This would probably be impossible in today's setting.

The preacher had bought an ample supply of dynamite sticks (cases) and it was the teenage boys responsibility to now clear the stumps from the future farm. The two teenagers had a long hand drill with a bit attached that was slightly larger than the stick of dynamite and about three feet long. This drill was manually operated. A hole would then be drilled through the dirt down beside the stump at an angle and as deep as possible. One stick of dynamite with a dynamite cap was attached and wires were attached to the stick of dynamite. The stick of dynamite and explosive cap was slowly pushed down into the hole made by the hand drill. The wires were stretched out about fifty feet where they had a battery awaiting. One wire was placed to one terminal and when all was clear the other wire was touched and "KABOOM", the stick of dynamite exploded and the stump usually came out of the ground as well. Some of the larger stumps required a second charge of dynamite to blow it out of the ground.

As dangerous as it may sound and probably was, the teenage boys knew the dangers and were always extremely cautious. Each teenager was the other's back up and watched to make sure every part of the dangerous operation was made to perfection. There was never an accident or a near accident. As many would say "This was just another day on the farm".

Another of the farm necessities was caring for the crop. Preacher Wiley had another farm where he and his family lived that was near Jonesville on the Little River and across the river from Jonesville. At one time in the spring, Preacher Wiley's son David and Bobby were given the necessary task of hand spraying the cotton crop for insects and worms which were especially bad that year. Boll Weevils were almost always a problem but this year was different. The insects and worms were about to destroy the crop. The two boys had backpack tank/sprayers and they mixed the poison up, poured it into the tanks and pumped the tanks up with an attached hand pump. They were required to walk each row of the cotton crop, hand spraying the cotton plants thoroughly. The problem with this job was that the preacher did not provide any type of facemask. Perhaps he did not think it was necessary.

Bobby stayed at the Wiley home while he and his friend and son of Preacher Wiley worked to spray a large field of cotton by hand. After two days of spraying, Bobby became deathly ill during the night; He threw up for hours from breathing the poison chemicals. No offer was made to take him to the doctor. Preacher Wiley and his wonderful wife simply came in prayed for him, gave him something for the nausea (probably Pepto Bismol) and went back to bed. Preacher Wiley was a Pentecostal preacher and practiced that prayer was the cure for anything. Although Bobby felt better the next morning he was still feeling the effects of inhaling the poisonous chemicals but still the two boys continued their job of spraying, now with bandanas over their faces. After a week, the two teenage boys now about fifteen years of age completed their assigned jobs and it was off to the next adventure.

One of those additional adventures was that of harvesting the crops. Preacher Wiley planted cotton of his farm where he lived. On the farm where the land clearing had taken place there was already a large number of acres that were cleared and in production. He raised corn on this farm. When harvest time came the ever-faithful Ford tractor was connected to a trailer and pulled down the rows of corn. The Wileys had a younger son who was about twelve and an older daughter who was about sixteen. The three Wiley children and Bobby would pull the ears of corn from the stalks, and toss them into the trailer. When the trailer was full, the load of corn would be taken to the barn where it was then unloaded by hand into the barn and stored for feed for their animals. This corn harvest was usually quickly followed by cotton harvest.

———————

CHAPTER 29

THIS PART OF LOUISIANA WAS unique in one respect when it came to boats. There were many families who lived and farmed near the Ouachita River and the other rivers that flowed into the Ouachita River. This created a problem for the school age children getting to and from school. Jonesville, Harrisonburg and Enterprise, Louisiana each had School Districts that utilized "SCHOOL BOATS".

These boats were covered or had enclosed cabins with seats arranged around the inboard motor. These boats with inboard engines were built for the specific purpose of serving the students and their education with transportation to and from school. They operated the same as school buses with safety requirements the same as the buses except that they operated on the rivers rather than on the streets and roads in the school district. So, the boats had one added feature that the buses did not have: they were required to have on board, life jackets for each of its passengers.

Each morning these school boats began their routes the same as the school buses. They would run the rivers making stops at each home on the river to pick up the school children. It was not uncommon for one of the parents to board the school boat for transportation into town to do their shopping. In this aspect, they acted as a taxi. Then in the afternoon after school was dismissed, they would return the students to their homes. Each of these towns that have been mentioned had special docks for the school boats, where they would dock and unload the children. There would be a school bus waiting for the school boat and the students would unload and the bus would complete the route to the school.

Many children spent their entire school life from first grade through high school, riding the school boat. The Johnson children experienced this unique method of school transportation for several years of their school education. This school boat system did not apply on the Little River and the Tensas River because they were narrow and were also shallow at times.

It was on one of the school boats that a memorable accident occurred. The school boat owner and operator had an older son who enjoyed playing tricks on the other passengers and students on the boat. One of his favorite tricks was to lay his hand on the arm or leg of another student and touch one of the sparkplugs on the engine. This was only twelve-volt DC current so there was no danger of serious injury, only a surprised little pulsating shock. The person touching the spark plug would feel a lesser jolt but the one who was being touched and was grounded received the greater jolt. On one of these occasions the operator's son slipped and accidently got his hand near the fan belt. His hand and fingers went between the belt and pulley and broke all his fingers and almost severed two of his fingers. His hand was deformed for life and he never had total use of the two fingers.

Another unique experience and practice in this farming area occurred during the crop harvest season. I am sure many other schools in farming regions had this same rule. Each fall at the harvest time, school would dismiss, usually at around one o'clock in the afternoon. Most farming enterprises were small family farms that required the assistance of the entire family. Harvest time was the most critical time of the year for the farmer.

When the weather was good, all the family was needed to help harvest the cotton. So, school districts were well aware of the need to harvest the crop as quickly as possible. The resulting policy allowed these school districts to dismiss early for crop harvest. This policy was changed later as farms and farming operations became more mechanized. There have now been chemicals developed that all but eliminate the grass and weeds in crops and planters that space plant the seeds, thereby eliminating the need for the strenuous labor of "chopping" or hoeing the crops. These chemicals are even specific to the type of crop being grown.

As the Johnson children grew older, they were never fearful of the water and they never had life jackets to carry with them on the boat. The Johnsons lived in several places where it was necessary to leave the car on one side of the river and use a boat to cross the river to their home. Farm to Market roads were simply not in every area of habitation as they are in modern society. It was during this time that Bobby received his hardship driver's license. He became the family chauffeur because his older brother Hubert had joined the Navy after graduating from high school. It was Bobby's job to take his younger brothers to school each day in Jonesville. Although the Johnsons lived several miles from Jonesville and across the river from Concordia Parish, they actually lived in Catahoula Parish and were required to attend school in Jonesville.

The Jonesville school district ended at the Ouachita River bridge and the Tensas River was also the Parish line for Concordia and Catahoula Parishes. The only school buses on the Concordia Parish side of the river went to Ferriday schools. The Johnson children would cross the river, which would put them now in Concordia Parish and about 100 yards from one of the Ferriday school bus stops, yet they were required to attend school in Jonesville. This created a tremendous dilemma for the school district since the distance from the river bridge to the Johnson home was several miles. The Johnson children were the only children in this situation with no school bus transportation.

The Catahoula Parish School simply could not, feasibly run a school bus into Concordia Parish for several miles (about ten) to pick up four children and transport them to and from school. Jack made arrangements with the Jonesville School District to solve the problem. The district would pay him for each mile; he had to transport each of his children to and from school. This arrangement not only saved the school district money but helped the finances of the Johnson family. It paid for the fuel and expenses plus additional funds for the time involved in the transporting of the children. This arrangement was similar to the contracts with school bus operators except on a smaller scale.

The School District wasn't aware that most of the school days, Bobby would actually be the driver that transported the children in his father's vehicle. Had they known that a fourteen or fifteen-year-old boy was the chauffeur of the other students the arrangement would have changed. They made the daily trips without any problems.

CHAPTER 30

—◆—

ANDREW HUBERT JOINED THE NAVY in 1955. The Korean War had ended and he spent much of his career in the Navy aboard the Aircraft Carrier, USS Hornet, as well as other vessels. His desire was also to learn a trade that would be beneficial to him after he was discharged from the Navy. He spent four years in the Navy. After he was discharged he went to Dallas to find work, and there he was employed by Ling Timco Vault Aircraft Company. He would later work for an air conditioner and heating company.

Hubert married Betty Jean Meadows in Dallas. Betty had been married and had several children. Hubert and Betty had two sons together. They later moved to Louisiana where Hubert worked for Delta Farms for several years as their supply and warehouse manager. Delta Farms was a large farming corporation that farmed several thousand acres near Jonesville. Hubert and his family spent several years in Louisiana and then moved back to Dallas where he worked as a maintenance supervisor for a building complex until he retired. Betty Jean Johnson died in Dallas in 1992.

As Bobby and Roy paddled their boat on the rivers or any of the various things they were occupied with, they were often talking of the future. Both boys realized that their future would be guided by an education and or training in a field where they could determine a good life and future. No doubt they liked the Louisiana area but both realized there were no opportunities for a good future in this area of Louisiana. They would have to leave for a different area to find a good job and realize their dreams. Most of the young men often began to work in the oil field, work offshore or work in south Louisiana and Texas. Both brothers wanted to be in a position to provide the very best for their families. They had experienced the difficulties of working hard with little money. Roy knew that he wanted to complete high school and try to go to college. Bobby realized that an education was very important for his future but he could not wait.

When Bobby was sixteen he began working for a local store owner between Jonesville and Ferriday. The store owner and his brother owned a large slaughter house where they maintained a busy schedule of not only slaughtering their own livestock and selling the meat at the store, but they also managed a packing company where they slaughtered animals for the area public. Bobby quickly learned the trade of butchering and assisted the store owner each day with butchering and wrapping the fresh meat for the customers.

Politics and the political races were always a thing of wonder and amazement in Louisiana. Louisiana has always been admired and despised for its politicians and what many outside the state described as "Dirty Politics". Two well-known politicians from Louisiana were the Long brothers, Huey P. Long and Earl K. Long. They were from nearby Winn Parish, Louisiana where a large contingent of Johnsons had resided since around 1850. The Long brothers were a household name with residents from all over Louisiana. Both brothers would eventually serve as governors of Louisiana and Huey P Long would make into the national political scene.

Involvement in politics was always a thing of wonder and amazement in Louisiana. The east central Louisiana area was no different. The Davis brothers, owners of the store and slaughter house were always involved in the local politics of Concordia Parish but were also in state politics as well. It was not unusual for any indi-vidual who was running for office in Concordia Parish to drop in to visit with the Davises.

On one such occasion a well-known politician visited the store to converse with his supporters, the Davis brothers. U.S. Congressman Otto Passman was a highly respected conservative Democrat from Monroe, Louisiana. He had begun his political career in 1946 and had moved up to the national level in politi-cal circles. The Concordia Parish area was part of Congressman Passman's district and the Davis brothers were supporters of the congressman. It was on one of those visits that Congressman Passman began to converse with Bobby about his education and his future. Congressman Passman told Bobby during the conversa-tion that, when he completed school he would be glad to try and help him get into one of the military academies.

After the visit and the conversation with Otto Passman, Mr. Davis quickly explained to Bobby what a great possibility this would be. Going to a military academy would be an opening for a great future. The only problem was that Bobby had already made up his mind that he was leaving school when he was seventeen and joining the military. His plans were to complete his educa-tion in the military. Bobby completed the summer job with the Davis brothers and at sixteen, just prior to his seventeenth birth-day, Bobby dropped out of school and worked for a few months as a roustabout in the oilfield.

He was waiting for the time when he would be seventeen and his parents could sign for him to enlist into the military. There he would study and complete his education and be trained for his fu-ture career. Bobby and Roy had often discussed their futures and what they each desired to achieve in the future for their lives. Roy was willing to finish his high school education and then pursue his future plans. Bobby decided he would take control of his future in a slightly different manner.

When they were old enough to enlist David Wiley, Bobby's friend and Pastor Wiley's son, joined the Army. Bobby joined the Air Force in January 1958. He was bused to Shreveport and sworn in at Barksdale Air Force Base. He then boarded a plane (his first) for his first airliner trip to Lackland Air Force Base, for his training. His friend and fellow companion in his farm work, David Wiley, joined the Army and was shipped out for his Basic Training.

After a year in the Army David Wiley was diagnosed with malignant brain tumors. He was treated in the army and when it was determined that the tumors were not responding to treatment, he was allowed to return home to be with his family during his remaining time. David Wiley died at home a few months later. Perhaps the breathing of the chemicals by the two boys had become the death sentence for David. Bobby never had any more problems after that first week of hand spraying the cotton fields.

CHAPTER 31

BOBBY WAS TRAINED AS A Crash Rescue and Firefighter in the Air Force and quickly set out to get his GED. Within a short time, he completed his GED and received his diploma from his high school in Jonesville. This would only be the beginning of his studies. He enrolled in courses offered by the Air Force in his career field to enhance his chances for advancement and for promotions. During his tour of duty in the Air Force Bobby was selected as Airman of the Month for the 3700th Civil Engineering Group.

While in the Air Force there were several international crises. First there was the Bay of Pigs invasion that was carried out by Cuban men who were trained in the U.S. and/or U.S. forces. When they invaded Cuba to overthrow Fidel Castro's government, they were promised that they would receive air support from the U.S. military. Their only support was from aircraft that had been converted to private ownership. However, when the invasion began, President J.F. Kennedy changed his mind and did not give them the much-needed U.S. military air support. The result was disastrous. The Cuban invaders of the Bay of Pigs were almost all captured or killed. Many would spend years in Cuban prisons as prisoners of Fidel Castro. Castro freed some of the men after $53 million in food and medical supplies were sent to Cuba.

When Fidel Castro overthrew the government of President Fulgencio Batista in Cuba in 1959, he immediately alienated the

United States by nationalizing American companies and seizing American-held land. President Dwight Eisenhower approved and initiated a plan to train and use Cuban refugees to overthrown Castro in March 1960, and John F. Kennedy assumed oversight of the plan when he became president. Training of the 1400-man group of exiles began in Florida and continued in Central America. The Bay of Pigs on the south coast of Cuba was chosen for the landing site because the area was sparsely populated and had an airfield large enough to land bombers to assure their success.

The invasion was disastrous from the start. Disguised aircraft bombers that were not from the U.S. military but privately owned and operated, did not succeed in destroying all of Cuba's aircraft, and the Cuban planes that were left attacked the ships that had brought the invasion force and drove them off before they could unload supplies. Instead of rebelling and joining the invaders as expected, the Cuban people supported Castro. The Cuban army was quickly deployed, and Castro himself arrived to oversee the defense. Although some of the invaders were successfully evacuated, more than 100 were killed and about 1,100 were captured. Only two hundred managed to escape capture.

The information and history given here is leading into another crisis in the world during Bobby's Air Force career.

At the end of World War II, Communist forces had moved into Germany and succeeded in beating the Allied forces (namely American) to Berlin. In the agreement signed by Allied and Russian leaders, the city of Berlin would be divided and controlled by the Communist government in the east and the U.S. would control the west with a corridor leading from West Berlin to West Germany.

The Communist government of the German Democratic Republic of East Germany in 1961 constructed the Berlin Wall. The wall separated the western and eastern parts of Berlin and effectively cut off West Berlin from East Berlin and the rest of Western Germany. Berlin was no longer an open city.

The newly constructed Berlin Wall included guard towers and an area that was fitted with anti-vehicle trenches and other military defenses. The wall was constructed to prevent East Germans from escaping into the Western Bloc-affiliated West Berlin, where they could in turn escape to Western European countries. There were often news clips of East Germans who were trapped behind the wall, trying desperately to escape to the West. Often the news clips would show the attempted escapes and the bodies of the escapees who were killed by the East German Guards. There were often news reports of successful escapes of individuals who had spent weeks or months devising plans of escape from East Berlin. The wall remained standing between 1961 and 1989. The wall was eventually re-opened after weeks of civil unrest in 1989. Germany was reunified in October 1990. The wall was then dismantled over a three-year period from 1989- 1992.

In August 1961, the Berlin Wall crisis began. Although East Germany was under communist or Russian control, agreements after World War II provided that the city of Berlin was to be a divided city. East Berlin would be under communist control and West Berlin would be under U.S or allied control. The city was essentially cut off from the rest of West Germany. There was an open corridor that the U.S. used to supply West Berlin. The agreement after World War II provided that this corridor would be a permanent open corridor for West Berlin which was under the control of the U.S. and its allies.

On August 30, 1961, President John F. Kennedy had ordered 148,000 Guardsmen and Reservists to active duty in response to Soviet moves to cut off allied access to Berlin. The Air National Guard's share of that mobilization was 21,067 individuals. Air National Guard units mobilized in October included 18 tactical fighter squadrons, 4 tactical reconnaissance squadrons, 6 air transport squadrons, and a tactical control group. On November 1, the Air Force mobilized three more ANG fighter interceptor squadrons. In late October and early November, eight of the tactical fighter units flew to Europe with their 216 aircraft in operation "Stair Step", the largest jet deployment in the Air Guard's history. Because of their short range, 60 Air Guard F-104 interceptors were airlifted to Europe in late November. The United States Air Forces in Europe (USAFE) lacked spare parts needed for the ANG's ageing F-84s and F-86s. Some units had been trained to deliver tactical nuclear weapons, not conventional bombs and bullets. They had to be re-trained for conventional missions once they arrived on the continent. The majority of mobilized Air Guardsmen remained in the US. [3]

During the crisis that developed the Soviet government decided to blockade any and all shipments into Western Berlin. The U.S. began airlifts to bring in supplies against the Soviet blockade and threats.

Bobby was due to be discharged from the Air Force in February, 1962. Several airmen from Bobby's 3700th Engineering Group were required to extend their enlistment. Bobby and his close friend "volunteered" to extend their enlistment for an additional nine months to November, 1962. Bobby had always stated that he enjoyed his military experience in the Air Force, so he accepted this extension with no remorse.

Another crisis developed in October, 1962, only one month before Bobby was to be discharged. In October, the Russian Government under Nikita Khrushchev decided to construct missile sites in Cuba and set up missiles with Russian troops as technical advisors. This would put the Russian missiles only ninety miles from the southern shores of the U.S.

In a televised speech, President John F. Kennedy announced that U.S. spy planes had discovered Soviet missile bases in Cuba.

---

3 Wikipedia, the free encyclopedia and Sources:bbc.co.uk

These missile sites were under construction but nearing completion. They housed medium-range missiles capable of striking a number of major cities in the United States, including Washington, D.C. President Kennedy announced that he was ordering a naval "quarantine" of Cuba to prevent Soviet ships from transporting any more offensive weapons to the island and explained that the United States would not tolerate the existence of the missile sites currently in place. The president made it clear that America would not stop short of military action to end what he called a "clandestine, reckless, and provocative threat to world peace."

What is known as the Cuban Missile Crisis actually began on October 15, 1962. On that day, the U.S. intelligence personnel analyzing U-2 spy plane data discovered that the Soviets were building medium-range missile sites in Cuba. The next day, President Kennedy secretly convened an emergency meeting of his senior military, political, and diplomatic advisers to discuss the ominous development. The group became known as ExCom, short for Executive Committee. After rejecting a surgical air strike against the missile sites and the possibility of this escalating into full nuclear war with the Soviet Union, ExCom decided on a naval quarantine and a demand that the bases be dismantled and missiles removed. On the night of October 22, Kennedy went on national television to announce his decision. During the next six days, the crisis escalated to a breaking point as the world tottered on the brink of nuclear war between the two superpowers.

From Share History:

On October 23rd, the quarantine of Cuba began, but Kennedy decided to give Soviet leader Nikita Khrushchev more time to consider the U.S. action by pulling the quarantine line back 500 miles. By October 24, Soviet ships en route to Cuba capable of carrying military cargoes appeared to have slowed down, altered, or reversed their course as they approached the quarantine, with the exception of one ship—the tanker *Bucharest*. At the request of more than 40 nonaligned nations, U.N. Secretary-General U Thant sent private appeals to Kennedy and Khrushchev, urging that their governments "refrain from any action that may aggravate the situation and bring with it the risk of war." At the direction of the Joint Chiefs of Staff, U.S. military forces went to DEFCON 2, the highest military alert ever reached in the postwar era, as military commanders prepared for full-scale war with the Soviet Union.

On October 25, the aircraft carrier USS *Essex* and the destroyer USS *Gearing* attempted to intercept the Soviet tanker *Bucharest* as it crossed over the U.S. quarantine of Cuba. The Soviet ship failed to cooperate, but the U.S. Navy restrained itself from forcibly seizing the ship, deeming it unlikely that the tanker was carrying offensive weapons. On October 26, Kennedy learned that work on the missile bases was proceeding without interruption, and ExCom considered authorizing a U.S. invasion of Cuba. The same day, the Soviets transmitted a proposal for ending the crisis: The missile bases would be removed in exchange for a U.S. pledge not to invade Cuba.

The next day, however, Khrushchev upped the ante by publicly calling for the dismantling of U.S. missile bases in Turkey under pressure from Soviet military commanders. While Kennedy and his crisis advisers debated this dangerous turn in negotiations, a U-2 spy plane was shot down over Cuba, and its pilot, Major Rudolf Anderson, was killed. To the dismay of the Pentagon, Kennedy forbid a military retaliation unless any more surveillance planes were fired upon over Cuba. To defuse the worsening crisis, Kennedy and his advisers agreed to dismantle the U.S. missile sites in Turkey but at a later date, in order to prevent the protest of Turkey, a key NATO member.

In mid-October, as the news was being made public, Bobby was called into headquarters and told he had orders to ship out immediately to Kessler Air Force in Mississippi. He was to leave ASAP and be at the base by midnight the next evening. There was very little time to prepare. Bobby packed his equipment and rushed to the base finance office to draw his travel pay. He serviced his car for the long drive. The time was now midday. Defcon (military high alert) had been initiated and was underway at all Military Bases.

Bobby received permission and decided to drive his car to his temporary duty assignment. This would take him through Baton Rouge where his brother Roy was attending L.S.U. Calculations indicated the drive would take at least 18 hours not including the stop for a visit with Roy.

After a brief visit with Roy, Bobby continued his trip to Biloxi with his sign-in deadline fast approaching. He had driven all night the previous night in order to meet the required check in time. When he arrived at Keesler A.F.B. the time was now near midnight. He had made the deadline with only minutes to spare

When Bobby arrived at Keesler A.F.B. in Biloxi, Mississippi, he was assigned to an Aircraft Crash Rescue unit at Keesler. The military was moving all its aircraft on southern bases to various locations, preparing for a possible attack by the Soviets. Some planes were being moved to selected public airports further away from the main bases and extra Crash Rescue Units were needed during the alert and while the blockade lasted or if war actually broke out.

After the Missile Crisis ended, Bobby returned to Reese Air Force Base in Lubbock. His discharge date was in November and he had spent two weeks on special assignment. He had accumulated over 60 days of leave time and the Air Force would only pay for 60 days. Bobby was told to take the leave or lose it. He chose to take the leave time and spent his last two weeks in the Air Force working at the Propane company to earn extra money.

While in the Air Force Bobby worked part time during his entire enlistment. When he was not on duty he was studying, or working. One of his first part time jobs was at the Base Dining (Chow)

Hall which was under civilian contract. He began at the butcher shop where he utilized his summer training as a butcher apprentice and store clerk. He later worked part time in the dining hall kitchen and then began working with a local butane and propane company, delivering propane to local farms and residences. He continued this work until his discharge.

Bobby spent four years and nine months in the Air Force and when he was discharged he applied for a civilian position with the Air Force in his career field of Aircraft Crash Rescue and Firefighter. He was later hired and began work at Reese Air Force Base, Lubbock, Texas where he had been stationed as an Airman. As a civilian employee, Bobby attended a local college to pursue a Bachelor of Science degree. One of his courses was Engineering Drawing.

He put this newly acquired educational skill to work at the base Fire and Crash Rescue Station. He began a large wall size map of the entire Reese A.F.B. layout. The map included all scale size buildings, streets, and even fire plugs and building symbols for hazardous material. The map would also include the Base ramp area and scale size aircraft. When the map was completed he received the highest award ever given to a civilian in the 3700th Engineering Group to which he was assigned. He received a Base "Outstanding Service Award".

Bobby continued his pursuit of education. While working, he continued to be enrolled in college. He majored in history and science and later received his degree from South Plains College near Lubbock, becoming the first of the lineage of John Evan Johnson to receive a college degree. He then began pilot training and trained for his private pilot's license which he received in 1977. He continued to amass college credits in Auto Cad Drafting, math, Spanish several continuing education courses and a Real Estate License.

Elizabeth Maudell ("Dell") was Jack's oldest daughter. She always possessed a motherly type of disposition and had many traits of her mother, Katherine Cecil. She married Donald Cagle who was a local young man from the Jonesville area. They were married in November of 1957 and they would have a family of three children.

In 1984, Dell became ill with what she and her family believed to be the flu. Dell was one who never liked going to the doctor and she dismissed the illness as being a temporary problem that would only last for a few days. Over the course of the next few weeks, her condition continued to deteriorate. When she went to the doctor, they immediately ruled out the flu. They began to run tests and when the lab work was completed the doctors delivered the crushing news. Elizabeth Maudell was diagnosed as having a rare form of Leukemia and it was in the last stages. Two weeks later Elizabeth Maudell Cagle succumbed to the disease.

The second daughter, and the fifth child, of Jack and Katherine Cecil was Ruth Evelyn Johnson. While the family was living in Clayton, Louisiana in 1963, Ruth met and married a man from the Ferriday-Clayton area. He was Clyde Green. They were married in 1963 and had one son. In 2004 Ruth became ill with a heart condition and within two years, Jack and Katherine Cecil's second daughter, died from heart failure. She was only sixty years of age.

Roy Lee was always the studious child in the family. Roy received his high school diploma just as he intended to do and enrolled in Louisiana State University in Baton Rouge. He later dropped out of school and began working in south Louisiana for a refinery as a Lab. Technician. He was drafted into the Army after the Vietnam conflict evolved into a full-scale U.S. involvement. This was after Congress had voted to implement the draft as forces were being increased for the Vietnam War. Roy spent two years in the Army. He was sent to Fort Leonard Wood, Missouri for Advanced Specialty Training. After he completed his training, he received orders for Korea. While in Korea, in a specially trained unit of soldiers, he was promoted quickly and excelled in his career field. He made several trips to Vietnam in a special capacity for the Army. After he was discharged, he began a career as a Lab Technician with an oil refinery in south Louisiana. Roy married Mickey Headrick and they had two children, Michael Dewayne Johnson and Nikki Michelle Johnson

Both young men were realizing their often-discussed dreams of having a good future for themselves and their families. Both realized the importance of education and both had strived to comply. They had lived in poverty and were determined to excel in each endeavor they faced in life. Bobby's daughter would excel in school and received a college degree in Business Finance and Accounting and Roy's son received a degree in Environmental Engineering.

Patsy Christine Johnson was Jack and Katherine Cecil's third daughter and sixth child. Patsy met and married a young man from Jonesville. His name was Gerald Prewitt. They were married in 1965 and they had three sons. Gerald loved to cook and grill.

The Johnson family had a family gathering each year in the spring and Gerald always looked forward to this event. He would get his fish fryer out and the family and friends always enjoyed a day of visiting, followed by a large meal and catfish fried up by Gerald. The meal was always followed by a softball game where the older men and women would be challenged by the younger members of the family.

In 1996, at the annual family gathering, Bobby and Roy were discussing with Gerald that he was pale and should visit the doctor. Gerald had mentioned in the conversation that he had not been feeling well. Gerald visited the doctor and he and his wife Patsy Christine received the stunning news. Gerald was diagnosed with stage four colon cancer and died a few months later. He left a wife and three sons.

———◆———

CHAPTER 32

YOU WILL RECALL THE MENTION of one of the Zattie Johnson's brothers, William, who had decided to remain in Mississippi when Zattie
decided to move to Arkansas. The year was eighteen thirty-eight.
William's father, Jeremiah and his family, along with Zattie. who
was then married and his family, had decided to move from the
Indian area of Mississippi. It was stated that (Jeremiah) "he just up
and decided to move to Union County, Arkansas".

Around one hundred thirty years later a tragic incident would
occur in Mississippi that would involve one of the descendants of
William Johnson, son of Jeremiah Johnson and brother of Zattie
Johnson. We will not identify this descendant of William Johnson.

On a warm, sticky, summer night in Philadelphia, Neshoba
County, Mississippi three civil rights workers were taken captive
and killed. Andrew Goodman, Michael Schwerner, and James
Chaney were murdered and buried in an earthen dam near
Philadelphia, Mississippi in Neshoba County, by a group of men
who opposed any advancement of the black people in the south.
Several years later, justice was meted out for seven men involved
in the horrible crime. All seven received severe sentences for the
crimes they had committed. One of the men who was involved in
these crimes was a descendant of William Johnson. We will not
identify this individual.

Below are the historical facts associated with the crimes.

Source: Share History

The remains of three civil rights workers whose disappearance on June 21st garnered national attention are found buried in an earthen dam near Philadelphia, Mississippi. Michael Schwerner and Andrew Goodman, both white New Yorkers, had traveled to heavily segregated Mississippi in 1964 to help organize civil rights efforts on behalf of the Congress of Racial Equality (CORE). The third man, James Chaney, was a local African American man who had joined CORE in 1963. The disappearance of the three young men led to a massive FBI investigation that was code-named MIBURN, for "Mississippi Burning."

Michael Schwerner, who arrived in Mississippi as a CORE field worker in January 1964, aroused the animosity of white supremacists after he organized a successful black boycott of a variety store in the city of Meridian and led voting registration efforts for African Americans. In May, Sam Bowers, the Imperial Wizard of the White Knights of the Ku Klux Klan of Mississippi, sent word that the 24-year-old Schwerner, nicknamed "Goatee" and "Jew-Boy" by the KKK, was to be eliminated. On the evening of June 16, two dozen armed Klansmen descended on Mt. Zion Methodist Church, an African American church in Neshoba County that Schwerner had arranged to use as a "Freedom School." Schwerner was not there at the time, but the Klansmen beat several African Americans present and then torched the church.

On January 20, Schwerner returned from a civil rights training session in Ohio with 21-year-old James Chaney and 20-year-old Andrew Goodman, a new recruit to CORE. The next day–June 21–the three went to investigate the burning of the church in Neshoba. While attempting to drive back to Meridian, they were stopped by Neshoba County Deputy Sheriff Cecil Price just inside the city limits of Philadelphia, the county seat. Price, a member of the KKK who had been looking out for Schwerner or other civil rights workers, threw them in the Neshoba County jail, allegedly under suspicion for church arson.

After seven hours in jail, during which the men were not allowed to make a phone call, Price released them on bail. After escorting them out of town, the deputy returned to Philadelphia to drop off an accompanying Philadelphia police officer. As soon as he was alone, he raced down the highway in pursuit of the three civil rights workers. He caught the men just inside the county limits and loaded them into his car. Two other cars pulled up filled with Klansmen who had been alerted by Price of the capture of the CORE workers, and the three cars drove down an unmarked dirt road called Rock Cut Road. Schwerner, Goodman, and Chaney were shot to death and their bodies buried in an earthen dam a few miles from the Mt. Zion Methodist Church.

The next day, the FBI began an investigation into the disappearance of the civil rights workers. On June 23, the case drew national headlines, and federal agents found the workers burned station wagon. Under pressure from Attorney General Robert F. Kennedy, the FBI escalated the investigation, which eventually involved more than 200 FBI agents and scores of federal troops who combed the woods and swamps looking for the bodies. The incident provided the final impetus needed for the 1964 Civil Rights Act to pass Congress on July 2, and eight days later FBI Director J. Edgar Hoover came to Mississippi to open a new Bureau office. Eventually, Delmar Dennis, a Klansman and one of the participants in the murders, was paid $30,000 and offered immunity from prosecution in exchange for information. On August 4, the remains of the three young men were found. The culprits were identified, but the state of Mississippi made no arrests.

Finally, on December 4th, nineteen men, including Deputy Price, were indicted by the U.S. Justice Department for violating the civil rights of Schwerner, Goodman, and Chaney (charging the suspects with civil rights violations was the only way to give the federal government jurisdiction in the case). After nearly three years of legal wrangling, in which the U.S. Supreme Court ultimately defended the indictments, the men went on trial in Jackson, Mississippi.

The trial was presided over by an ardent segregationist, U.S. District Judge William Cox, but under pressure from federal authorities and fearing impeachment, he took the case seriously. On October 27, 1967, an all-white jury found seven of the men guilty, including Price and KKK Imperial Wizard Bowers. Nine were acquitted, and the jury deadlocked on three others. The mixed verdict was hailed as a major civil rights victory, as no one in Mississippi had ever before been convicted for actions taken against a civil rights worker.

In December, Judge Cox sentenced the men to prison terms ranging from three to 10 years. After sentencing, he said, "They killed one nigger, one Jew, and a white man. I gave them what I thought they deserved." None of the convicted men served more than six years behind bars.

On June 21, 2005, the forty-first anniversary of the three murders, Edgar Ray Killen was found guilty of three counts of manslaughter. At eighty years of age and best known as an outspoken white supremacist and part-time Baptist minister, he was sentenced to 60 years in prison.

———

CHAPTER 33

THERE IS AN OLD SAYING that "the third child is always prone to accidents or getting sick". Whether this saying is true or not is a subject for debate. Yet it has been true in many cases and this was found to be true in the Johnson Family. Bobby was the third child and he was destined for many calamities in his life from illnesses to accidents.

From the time, Bobby was small, he was always being hurt or injuring himself in some way and many times in strange ways. Sometimes these injuries occurred from being involved in situations with his older brother, Andrew Hubert, or his older sister Elizabeth Maudell "Dell".

When Bobby was four years old his family was living near Enterprise, Louisiana. This was also the home where Bobby was born December 28, 1940. The family did not have electricity in the home and relied on a wood stove to cook on and a wood heater during the winter. Bobby was playing near the wood heater when he lost his balance and both knees hit the red-hot heater, instantly producing third degree burns on both knees. It would take several weeks for him to recover from this accident. This was the first of many accidents that he could remember in a long list of illnesses and accidents.

The farm had an old barn with what was called a corncrib. The corncrib had a large wooden door that separated it from the rest of the barn and had a wooden floor. Bobby and his older brother Hubert were in the barn when the door came loose from the hinges and fell hitting Bobby and trapping him under the heavy wooden door. The older brother could not lift the door and ran to get his mother and tell her what had happened. When they began to lift the door off Bobby, it was discovered that nails protruding from the door had stuck into his back and impaled Bobby to the door.

Luckily none of the nails had done major damage. After removing Bobby from under the door he was discovered not to have any major injuries. His mother applied her favorite medicine to the nail injuries. She always had a supply of kerosene on hand to start the fires in the stove or heater so she applied the kerosene to stop the bleeding and probably completed caring for the injuries with a healthy application of Merthiolate for bacteria. Life continued. Her medications always seemed to be a good treatment. They darn sure burned but were effective. All the children were living proof that their mother was a very good Nurse and Medical Practitioner.

The family was living on property that was known as "The Guice Place". Jack would occasionally be called on by the property owner to help with various things which most often involved assisting in locating and rounding up the livestock that roamed in the piney woods and forest areas owned by the family. Billy Guice was the son of the property owner and later became a school teacher and eventually, Superintendent of Schools. Hundreds of acres of the property were forest land. Billy Guice was a unique individual in the fact that he had lost one arm. Yet Billy was an excellent horseman. He could ride horses and rope cattle almost as well as someone with both arms.

It was on one of these cattle searches when something happened that would always be remembered by the older Johnson children. Billy always brought his dogs with him to help locate the cattle and assist in herding the cattle. There were large numbers of wild hogs that roamed the piney woods and hills -so-called because most of the timber in the forest was Loblolly Pine. The dogs found one group of wild hogs and went into aggressive mode. One of the wild boars defended himself with his large tusks (which were common in the wild hog population) and began an attack on the dogs.

During the attack, one of the dogs was successfully struck by the boar and received a large gash or cut. Billy and Jack came riding in carrying the injured dog on the horse. Billy asked Katherine Cecil for a needle and thread and they sewed the injured dog's large cut. No one can remember if the dog survived the injury and the sutures placed there with a needle and thread or not. It is a pretty good bet that he did survive.

The place where the family washed their clothes was a short distance away from the house near a large pond and near the Ouachita River. Water would be carried from the river to fill large washtubs for their mother to wash. One tub was placed on some rocks and a fire was built to heat the water to wash the cloths. One of the tubs was a large oval shaped tub.

One day when Bobby, Hubert and their sister Dell were playing near the pond, the two older siblings came upon a super idea. Why not put Bobby in the large oval tub in the pond and push him off into the pond? This could be their little brother's boat. The tub was big enough to act as a boat for the little brother, but they never considered that (1) Bobby couldn't swim, nor (2) how to get him back to shore. Then there were other unanswered questions that needed to be considered. Could a wash tub really float as well as a boat? After they pushed him off and he drifted farther into the pond, they then realized the dilemmas. They tried to instruct Bobby to use his hands as a paddle and paddle himself back to shore. Then they realized another problem.

With its flat bottom, the tub was not as stable as a boat. As Bobby began to follow instructions, the tub began to rock dumping Bobby into the deep water of the pond. Both siblings jumped into the water to rescue their little brother before disaster struck. They made the rescue and had an answer to their perceived debate about the washtub being a good boat. Was it a good boat? No!!! It was not to be used as a boat. Only use it for its intended purpose, "To Wash Clothes". The tub was not a good boat and one should never try to make a sailor out of your little brother even if he was a willing participant.

You have read about the flood of 1949. After the flood and the Johnson family had moved back into their home, Bobby was playing on the back porch with his dog. He was barefoot. He stuck a splinter from the wooden floor under the nail of his big toe. This was a large splinter and almost covered the full width of his toe and went completely under the nail and into the flesh at the back of the nail. Bobby didn't tell his mother but went in and retrieved one of his father's razor blades and a pair of tweezers. He would perform his own surgery required to remove the splinter. After cutting through the nail with the razor blade, he discovered that he could not remove the splinter and needed to tell his mother. She took one look and knew Bobby needed to go to the doctor.

Jack was working so she needed to go to her niece's home and ask her to take them to the doctor. The families left their cars across the river near Enterprise. They crossed the river and went to Jonesville to the doctor. The doctor removed Bobby's nail and the splinter, and bandaged the now nail-less toe. Bobby would be okay in a few days and off to his next adventure.

When they left the farm near Enterprise a few months later and went to Greensboro, North Carolina, they lived near a tobacco warehouse and auction (which has already been mentioned). There was one part left unmentioned. Here is the rest of the story.

On the weekends, there were always tobacco auctions where the farmers would sell their cured tobacco. This meant that there were vendors with free hot dogs and drinks. Bobby, Hubert and Roy would pay a visit so they, too, could receive the free hot dogs and cokes. After the auctions were over, they would then search the area and pick up drink bottles that had been discarded. They would then sell the empty bottles to one of the local stores for the deposit refund. All drink bottles were of glass and were reusable. You always paid a deposit on the bottle when you bought a drink, which was then refundable when the empty bottle was returned.

One weekend after the crowds had left, the boys were searching for bottles when Bobby who was barefoot, struck a broken bottle with his foot. The side of his big toe received a large cut that severed an artery. The boys struggled to get home as fast as they could and with each heart beat a stream of blood would come from Bobby's toe. This was the same toe that had received the splinter removal surgery only about a year before. When they arrived home, Bobby's mother took out her favorite medicine, (kerosene) and poured this on the cut, soaked a bandage in the kerosene and tightly bandaged the toe to stop the bleeding. A week or so later he was as good as new again and awaiting the next unexpected accident of many in his life.

You already know that in 1952 the Johnsons returned to Louisiana from North Carolina after being there almost two years. They eventually moved to Jena, Louisiana to be near Katherine Cecil's sister while Jack worked in Harvey, Louisiana, across the Mississippi River from New Orleans. One morning Bobby went to the bathroom and discovered that he was urinating blood. When he looked in the mirror his face was horribly swollen. He ran to his mother who could see his face and explained the blood issue. Katherine Cecil quickly took him to the doctor because she realized and understood that he had a major kidney problem. After seeing the doctor, the doctor told Katherine that she needed to rush Bobby to the Charity Hospital in Alexandria, Louisiana because he had serious poisons in his system that could cause death if not attended quickly. The doctor prepared all the paper work for the Alexandria hospital where Bobby was taken and he was immediately admitted.

After extensive tests were run, Katherine was informed that Bobby had a severe case of albumin in the kidneys. The presence of albumin in the urine (albuminuria) indicates malfunction of the kidneys, and may accompany kidney disease or heart failure. A person with severe renal disease may lose as much as 20 to 30 grams of plasma proteins in the urine in one day and death is also a real possibility.

Bobby remained in the hospital as the medical problem was treated and brought under control. After one week, the nurses discovered that he had developed a blockage of the colon since he had been in the hospital and Bobby had failed to complain about this until the pain was so severe that his mother made the situation known to the doctors. This issue was immediately corrected with medication and enemas.

Bobby was never allowed out of bed while in the hospital where he remained for two weeks. Jack rented a home in Belle Chase, Louisiana for the family to move to south Louisiana. The problem was now Bobby's illness. A request was made for the doctor to allow Bobby to transfer to the Charity Hospital in New Orleans. The doctor released Bobby with strict instructions that he was to remain in bed for two months and visit the hospital in New Orleans each week or until they were told different. After two months Bobby, had completely recovered and never had the kidney problem again.

One year later Bobby began to have severe pain in the right abdomen. He was taken to the hospital in New Orleans where he underwent emergency surgery for appendicitis. When the doctors performed the surgery, they discovered that he did not have appendicitis. There must be something else that was causing the severe pain. They enlarged the incision for exploratory surgery and still found nothing. They performed the appendectomy but never determined what was causing the severe abdominal pain. Final results were an appendix removal and a larger than normal scar from the surgery. Recovery was rapid and the family now awaited the next crisis or accident. There are just too many to account for in this narrative.

CHAPTER 34

———◆———

THERE IS ONE CHILD THAT has been mentioned only with the list of children of Jack and Katherine Cecil. One reason for this is that Jackie Faye was born nine years after her sister Patsy was born. This was a time when the older children had already left home or were preparing to leave. Andrew Hubert was already in the Navy; Bobby was awaiting his seventeenth birthday when he planned to join the Air Force; and Elizabeth Maudell was to be married in a few months and was ready to begin her family. Katherine Cecil was now forty years of age and was surprised with the welcome news that another child was on the way. Jackie Fay was born on June 27, 1956.

A few miles away from the Jonesville area, where Jack and Katherine Cecil received the news of a new baby on the way, is the town of Harrisonburg, where Katherine Cecil's youngest sister Ethel lived. Ethel had three children and her youngest was now twelve years of age. Ethel was not going to let her sister Katherine Cecil, outdo her. She received news that she was also expecting another baby. Jackie Fay and Donnie Wayne's birthdays are less than one month apart. Donnie Wayne was born on July 20, 1956.

Jackie Faye was also a studious child and would continue her education after graduating from high school. Jackie was married in 1976 and she and her husband would have two daughters. She also studied shorthand and then Hotel Management. She worked for several years for the government of Catahoula Parish. She worked for several years at a correction facility as a teacher and instructor in computer programs. Today Jackie Fay is teaching handicapped children at a local school in Louisiana.

The Holiday season was always very special to the Johnson family. Thanksgiving was always enjoyed by all and was always a time for the family to gather. Although Christmas was always very special and the Johnson children looked forward to Christmas, they never received lots of gifts as other families did. The children always received one special gift and perhaps several small gifts, but Katherine Cecil had started one tradition that the family always looked forward to.

Although there was usually no money for a lot of gifts, the children knew that they had the greatest gift of all and that was the love of their father and mother. Bobby once did a Christmas devotion and entitled it: "**The Greatest Gift In A Brown Paper Bag**."

This was because of a family tradition that was started by their mother.

Each Christmas, Katherine Cecil would buy several brown paper bags, one for each of her children. She wrote each child's name on the bag and made it ready for the children when they woke up on Christmas morning. She always bought mixed nuts in the shells, oranges, tangerines, apples, hard candy and peppermint sticks. In each bag, she would place one apple, one orange, one tangerine, one handful of nuts, one handful of hard candy and a peppermint stick. She made sure that each child received the same amount of each thing she placed in the brown paper bag. The children always looked forward to seeing their bag made ready especially for them, with their name on it.

Although each child knew what would be in the bag, there was never a Christmas morning that they did not have a smile on their face when they saw the bag. They knew with certainty that their mother had prepared each of the bags with as much love that any mother could have for their child. Each orange, each apple, each tangerine, each handful of nuts, each handful of hard candy and each peppermint stick was prepared with tremendous love. They were sure there was some sadness also, because she could not give her children the nice gifts that other families gave their children, but they all knew that all she could give was given with tremendous and equal love to all her children and she always prepared a special meal.

When Bobby was discharged from the Air Force he became engaged to a beautiful young lady. She was attending Texas Tech and studying for a degree in Education. Sara Beth Deavours and Bobby were married in June of 1964 and she began teaching at the school she had graduated from, near Lubbock, Texas. The second year of their marriage they traveled from Lubbock to Clayton, Louisiana for the Christmas holiday, where the Johnsons now lived and Jack ran a gas station.

On Christmas morning when the family got up, Bobby looked over near the Christmas tree and there was a brown paper bag with his name on it, but another bag had now been added to the row of brown paper bags. There beside Bobby's bag of an apple, orange, tangerine, nuts, candy, and peppermint stick was a brown paper bag for his wife, Sara Beth. His mother had not forgotten. Bobby had been away in the Air Force for almost five years and was now working for the Air Force as a civilian, but he looked expectantly for **"The Greatest Gift in A Brown Paper Bag".** This gift was "A Mother's Love" for her children. Although they were now adults, his mother had not forgotten.

———◆———

CHAPTER 35

AROUND 1968, BOBBY AND SARA visited Bobby's parents in Clayton. This was one of many trips that would be taken over the next thirty-eight years. However, this trip would be one of significance in the lives of all of Jack and Katherine's family.

Jack had just received some great and unexpected news. His half-sister in El Dorado, Arkansas had informed him that there was news about the adopted brother, Almer. They had not seen their brother since 1918, when he was only an infant and adopted by John and Corine Temples. Neither had they heard, nor did they know, where the Temples family and their adopted brother had moved to. How they had received this information is now unknown.

Almer was living in Ft. Worth, Texas and had several children with the Temple name. Jack asked Bobby and his wife, Sara, if they would check this information out. Bobby and his wife would be traveling through Ft. Worth on their return trip to Lubbock and when they went through Ft. Worth, they called the phone number that Jack had been given. Sure enough, Almer Johnson Temples answered the phone.

The conversation was somewhat strained and difficult at first as Bobby explained who he was, and why he was calling this stranger. Almer, likewise, thought the conversation and the resulting information and questions were shocking and difficult. As Bobby and Almer asked each other questions, and answered questions, they were filled with excitement and expectations. Each awaited the answer to never before asked questions and the need and desire for information that would be somewhat life changing for each of them and their families. After several minutes of conversation and discussion about the family, Almer asked Bobby and Sara to please come to his home so they could become acquainted and converse more.

Almer knew that he had lived in El Dorado, Arkansas as a child and was supposed to have family in and near El Dorado, Arkansas. He knew that he was adopted and apparently, he was the one who had begun the search for the missing link to his family. It was not immediately known if Almer's adopted parents had always told him that he was adopted and if he had always known of his family of fifty years prior. It was known that no contact had ever been made and this was the beginning of life changing revelations.

Almer was enthusiastic as he questioned Bobby about his brother and his family. News was relayed to Jack that Almer was indeed in Ft. Worth, Texas and wanted very much to establish relations. Almer and Jack made contact and within a few months the two brothers were re-united. Almer was brought up to date on his Johnson family. After fifty years, the brothers would begin a relationship that would again bind the loose ends of the family history for each of the brothers and each family. Almer and his wife were reunited with his sister in El Dorado and his brother George who was living in Mississippi. Over the course of the next several years, Almer, Jack, and George would visit often.

George, Jack and Almer visited the area where they were born in Bradley County, Arkansas and each brother saw the old places that were forever a part of their early life. Jack relived all the early years when his family struggled to remain together only to be forced to take actions that would divide the family. Their father, Hubert Lee, had so desperately struggled to provide for his children and keep them together, then only to be forced apart by the circumstances beyond his control. Jack and George explained to their brother, Almer, all the reasons why they were forced to be separated and each brother relived those times with very different memories.

Jack and George's life and memories returned to a difficult struggle and sadness as their mother died from giving birth to two beautiful sons. Then there was the sadness only a few months later as one of their twin brothers who had suffered from health issues since his birth, struggled to live and then only to lose his battle with life.

Jack and George relived those months that followed and their father's battle to provide for his remaining family, with little money and little work to provide for them. Jack and George recalled that fateful day when the family helplessly watched their home burn to the ground. Jack had seen firsthand his father's anguish when he realized that he would have to separate his six children to give them a chance at life.

The brothers visited the small Moro Bay Baptist Church that was still standing. This was the church where his mother's last rites were held. They visited the cemetery where she was placed and where a few months later her infant son was placed beside her. They discussed how the children were sent to live with different relatives and how their half-sister had taken them in cared for them as a mother, though she was just a teenager and a newlywed, little more than a child herself.

Then Jack took the two brothers to the banks of the Ouachita River and the area where he and his father had constructed a large raft to carry them away from the bitter memories of Bradley County to a new destination in life. He explained to the brothers about their travels down to Ouachita River and their eventual home in Jonesville where their father Hubert Lee would lose his life only seven years later.

Almer was just a baby and would never have any recollection of those difficult days that led up to their separation. His memories were of a family who saw the Johnson family's plight and graciously took in a baby boy that they would care for and raise and love him as their own son. Almer's memories of his childhood were quite different from those that Jack and George spoke of. His adopted family had moved from Arkansas to Texas and life had been one of happy memories. His adoptive father had been able to find work and provided for his family and their needs very well.

The fifty years of separation were now over and the ties were now restored that would bind them closely over the next few years. Almer and his wife had several children who lived in and near Ft. Worth. Almer and his wife moved to the Arkansas area and lived there only a short time before their deaths in the late 1970s. Both are buried in the Marsden Cemetery in Bradley County, Arkansas near a large number of Johnson family members.

Jack's older brother, Roy Lee, died in Greensboro in June of 1961 at the age of fifty-five years. George Johnson died in Rolling Fork, Mississippi in 1988, and he and his wife, Nell, are buried in the Mounds Cemetery in Rolling Fork, Mississippi.

CHAPTER 36

———◆———

As JACK BEGAN TO GET older and heavy physical or manual labor became impossible, he accepted a job as night watchman at a large
sawmill. Today we would call this type of employment, night security. After spending several years working at night for the mill, he
changed jobs. He then began working for a large farming corporation near Jonesville. The Delta Plantation owned and farmed
several thousand acres of land in the Jonesville area of Louisiana.
Jack's job was to drive around the plantation and check the equipment and storage facilities for the corporation. At specified locations, he would punch a clock to verify that he had checked the
facilities and that they were secure.

Central Louisiana has always been well known for its many
churches and church revivals. Most often these were held in large
tents that were set up by the traveling preacher. Usually these revivals were held in the summer and fall and the Johnson family would
attend these revivals if at all possible. This was during the 1950s
and Jimmy Swaggart was becoming well known as a teenager who
was already a preacher. He was becoming well known throughout
the Pentecostal circles, especially central Louisiana.

The Ferriday and Jonesville, Louisiana area produced some
other well-known individuals other than those in the political are-
na. Some of those were involved in music entertainment, as well
as the church. Jimmy Swaggart was from this area of Louisiana.

This in itself was phenomenal for a teenager to know the teachings of the Bible so well, but most of all in the style that this young man delivered his sermons. Jimmy would always credit his mother and father as being influential in his Christian life, but he always credited his grandmother as being very influential in his call to the ministry.

There were also Jimmy's famous cousins, Mickey Gilley and Jerry Lee Lewis. As children, the Johnsons were most acquainted with Jerry Lee Lewis and Jimmy Swaggart. This was also the time when Jerry Lee Lewis was trying to break into the country music and rock and roll music scene. Jerry Lee would go around to various churches in the Vidalia, Ferriday and Jonesville area and play the piano and sing. One of Bobby's school friends was Johnnie Edwards. Johnnie married one of Jerry Lee's relatives. (either a sister or cousin) Johnnie later joined Jerry Lee's tours as one of his bus drivers. Jerry Lee would become a well-known Rock and Roll music star. Not to be outdone, was his cousin Mickey Gilley, who also became a well-known and popular country music star.

Throughout Jack's life he had always attended church faithfully. We have already mentioned that Jack was always dependent on prayer and his involvement in church to sustain him. In difficult times and in times of ill health he relied on his faith and prayer. Most of the Johnson children could never remember a television in their home when they were growing up. Jack and Katherine Cecil both believed that there were too many programs on TV that they did not want their children to be exposed to. Also, until the mid-1970s, most Pentecostal preachers preached against the evils of television. The church would later ease up on some of the restrictions that had been an instrumental part of the church doctrine.

When he finally made the decision to purchase a television, Jack convinced himself that it was only so he could watch the news and the weather. Well! A little western occasionally such as Bonanza or Maverick isn't so bad, so he included these weekly shows to his "to watch" list. So, this was Jack's experience with the television. I'm sure his news, weather and westerns gradually evolved into some of the other shows but true to his word he would never be an addicted television watcher and watch the other shows that most people felt were permissible but to Jack they were offensive to his Christian standards.

Jack would not allow his children to attend the movies when they were young. This changed as the children became older and this was not frowned on by the church as much as it once had been. In nineteen forty-seven Jack and his family were living in Ferriday. You have already read of the pick-up truck without doors and the accident that occurred when Jack dodged the cow and threw his wife and baby out the side of the pick-up.

It was during this time that Jack's brother, Hazel, visited the family for a few days. Hazel, as you recall, was a drifter and would occasionally come by unexpectedly to visit. These visits were rare and occasionally one of the brothers from North Carolina would notify Jack that Hazel or Troy had been by to visit. Or Jack would notify other members of the family if one of the brothers showed up at his home. Troy was the other brother of Jack who was also a drifter.

It was on this visit in nineteen forty-eight had that Hazel talked Jack into going to a cowboy movie at the local theater. Remember that Jack would not allow his children to attend movies and Jack abided by the same rule. After all, the church frowned on the sin of attending the movie theaters and Jack was a staunch believer in the church and obedient to the church's teachings. The movie visit was just a final outing before Hazel again left and would not be heard from for months or perhaps years.

When Hazel left, after he and Jack saw the cowboy flick, Jack was convicted for his failure to be obedient to his belief, and that it was wrong and to him a sin. Jack told Katherine Cecil of his failure and they went into prayer for this perceived failure to seek forgiveness. This was the type of individual Jack was. If he believed he had failed God in any way, then he needed to seek forgiveness and he would suffer from tremendous guilt until he "Made It Right With God". This was true any time that Jack felt he had done something that was not pleasing to God. But simply saying "God forgive Me" was not Jack's nature. He would go into a prayer mode in which he would continue to pray and "Seek God" until he felt that the burden had been lifted from him.

Jack took this attitude into his lifestyle. He was a prayer warrior. He seemed to thoroughly enjoy praying. Often his prayers would last for thirty minutes or even longer. It was not uncommon for Jack to be heard several times a day simply praising God or saying "Thank you God". This was his lifestyle and he was never embarrassed to express the fact that he was a Christian. He was never boisterous but always humble.

Jack had always been a drinker of coffee, for all his adult life. He would drink coffee in the morning, in the evening, and any time in between. During the early years of his Christian life, there would occasionally be a preacher who would preach against drinking coffee because it contained caffeine and was perceived to be addictive, therefore should be forbidden by the church. Jack would be obedient to the message and restrain from drinking coffee for a time but then he would again take up his habit of drinking his beloved cup of coffee.

Jack had suffered from indigestion for many years. He was diagnosed as having ulcers and when the gastric problems would commence he would go on his special diet of milk and crackers and soft food until he felt that the problem was solved and with him very seldom going to visit a doctor. In 1998, Jack began to suffer with his gastric problems again. However, this time his special diet didn't relieve the symptoms as it had in the past. His indigestion persisted and he even began to have some difficulty swallowing. He went to the doctor for an examination and tests were made to determine what the issue was. Was it the ulcers that had gotten worse or was it something in his diet that was creating the problem?

When the tests were completed and the results came back, Jack received some bad news. The indigestion and acid reflux problems over the years had caused an erosion in the lower esophagus and this had progressed into esophageal cancer. Jack was now stage four and was given about six months to live.

One would immediately think that the first thing Jack would do with his history of prayer would be to begin praying for God to heal him. After all he had prayed this prayer many times over the years of his Christian life. He had many times prayed for himself, his children and for others who would come to him for special prayer.

Instead of praying for God to heal him, this is what Jack prayed. "God, I am not going to ask You to heal me. If You do heal me then I will praise You for it. If You do not heal me then I will continue to praise You." Then Jack added a very unusual addition and request to his prayer. He said "God I will pray and ask You not to let me suffer more than I can bear it".

This may not sound unusual until you hear the rest of the story. Jack had a very low tolerance for pain. I will exaggerate some for the inclusion of humor. Jack could stick a splinter or in many cases a thorn in his finger and you would think he had broken his finger because of the way he would carry on and complain. When Katherine Cecil would get a needle to remove the splinter or thorn he would begin saying "ouch, ouch", before she had even begun the process of removing the irritant object. As I said, there is some exaggeration there, but the fact remains that Jack had a low tolerance for pain. Thus, the reason that he was praying "God please do not allow me to suffer very much" during his remaining months. "Don't let me suffer more than I can bear".

Jack didn't undergo any chemotherapy treatments during his bout with esophageal cancer. He relied almost totally on prayer. As the months passed he digressed to the point where he could no longer eat solid foods.

Katherine Cecil had some health issues as well. She now had a heart condition that would progress to the point where she was confined to a wheelchair or bed. In the months that would pass, both husband and wife continued to live at home with assistance from medical care givers and their daughters, who visited daily to assist them. Finally, their conditions were such that they could no longer remain in their home. Their health issues were at a point at the turn of the year from 1998 to 1999, that they both were placed in a nursing home.

Two months after going to the nursing home Katherine Cecil had begun to have problems swallowing, possibly caused by a small stroke. She was placed into a hospital for a surgical procedure that was for a feeding tube to assist her in eating. She would never leave the hospital. Her heart problems surfaced and she went into cardiac arrest. All of her children were called in and when her last child entered the room, one of the daughters told their mother that "everyone is now here". Katherine Cecil Johnson passed away in the presence of her children in February, 1999, just a month short of her eighty third birthday.

Remember that Jack had been given six months to live. We are now well past the six months and although his condition was not improving he was still praying and making the best of his time with his wife and family.

Over the next nine months of nineteen ninety-nine Jack would relive his travels down the Ouachita River at the age of twelve. He stated that he wished he had taken the time to travel that route again.

His sons would visit and take Jack for rides to places that he decided he would like to see. One of those places that he visited on two occasions was to show his sons where his father Hubert Lee Johnson was buried in an obscure cemetery not far from the Black River and across the river from Jonesville.

Zattie May "Jack" Johnson died of esophageal cancer in September 1999. Not six months as the doctors had stated but almost eighteen months after his diagnosis. During those almost eighteen months Jack continued to pray. All the children visited their father often. Bobby had visited his father and mother often on the weekends when they were in the Nursing Home. After Katherine Cecil's death, he visited his father regularly, almost every weekend for several months.

Jack's other children were visiting regularly and an amazing thing was discussed among the children. Jack had prayed that God "not allow him to suffer". God had answered his prayer. The children would realize that Jack had not complained of major pain during his one and one half years of suffering from a very painful form of cancer. The prayer that he had prayed had been answered from a faithful God. Jack had been a faithful servant of God and had lived out his promise to serve God until his death. God had been faithful and answered Zattie May "Jack" Johnson's prayer and did not allow him to suffer with unbearable pain.

One of the central themes of the Bible and Christianity is based on how one lives his or her life after accepting Christ as Savior. One must conclude that Jack and Katherine Cecil certainly touched many lives in a very positive way in their Christian service.

When Jack passed away, his church service, honoring his life was held in the Pentecostal church where he and his wife had attended for many years. The church was filled with family, friends, fellow church members and people who remembered and wanted to honor the family with their presence. Here was a man who was lying in state, in a church where he had served. Here was a man who was uneducated and was never one who stood out in a crowd.

Yet here was a man who had taken an early stand to raise his family in a Christian environment and had stood fast to his beliefs, all his Christian life.

Now in attendance for his memorial was a church full of people whose lives were somehow touched by this uneducated yet humble man. Here was evidence of one who called himself a Christian and strived to live a life that was not only conducive to the Christian ethics but one who unknowingly had affected so many lives. Many of these people were individuals with whom he had prayed for their healing and God's blessing on their lives. Many of these people were individuals with whom he and his wife had served and were acquainted in the Church circles. The lives of their children had been influenced by them. In the future, other lives would be influenced by those who had been blessed by this humble, faithful servant of God.

Zattie May "Jack" Johnson's many prayers through the years had been answered by the lives he touched and his dedication to serving his God was evident. Here was the proof.

CHAPTER 37

BOBBY'S WIFE OF THIRTY-EIGHT YEARS, Sara Beth, died two years after Jack died. She had been a dedicated school teacher for thirty-seven of those years. She had missed only two years of teaching when their two children were born, so she had thirty-four years of teaching credit toward her retirement. She was determined to get her thirty-five years of teaching toward her retirement.

Sara had been diagnosed with colon cancer in nineteen ninety-three and after surgery and chemotherapy had been in remission. In the year two thousand she again began to have pain in the lower back and abdomen. She was told that the cancer had returned. The MRI revealed that not only had the colon cancer returned but a malignant tumor was attached to the exterior of her colon and had spread to her kidney, liver and her inner spine. She was taken into surgery but the efforts to remove to tumor were not successful. After she had major surgery in July of two thousand she again started the regiment of chemotherapy. Teaching school had been her life's ambition and she was totally dedicated to her career. She was just beginning her thirty fifth year and she could retire. Sara would teach until the time she had to leave for the treatments. She would schedule those treatments so she would not have to leave her classroom. Almost always, she would undergo her chemotherapy treatments in the afternoon and then would return the next day to her classroom. Her fellow teachers took turns filling in for her in her classroom during her few hours of absence.

Throughout the next few months she now began to plan on her forced retirement because of the cancer which was only being managed. She was able to teach to the holiday season of her thirty fifth year. With her sick leave and her accumulated leave time, she would be able to make it until January and her retirement date with thirty-five years. She could retire in January before classes began again. Sara's health continued to deteriorate. She wanted to remain at home and Bobby became her care-giver for the next ten months.

Sara was also a Christian and had been since she was only a teenager. She would often sit and pray for relief as the disease continued to destroy her body. She passed away on November first, two thousand two in the presence of her husband and children.

In two thousand six, Bobby met a legal professional who lived in Austin, Texas. Donna Elaine had once lived in Monroe where she had worked in banking and auditing before entering the legal profession. Bobby drove to Austin to meet the lady that he had met on eHarmony. They had been a match in many areas on the criteria submitted to eHarmony in their required questionnaire. After their meeting, they realized they both had many compatible qualities, including church attendance and travel. Bobby quickly realized that his education and average intellect would be put to the test. Donna was extremely intelligent so Bobby would have to rely on his life skills and common sense to win her over. They were married in two thousand seven. In the future, she would often assist Bobby in his writing ventures.

Bobby would need her expertise and her vast knowledge of the intricacies involved in word processing as he compiled his family's genealogy, published his first book "High on The Mountain" and prepared for his next book, "Clan-Destiny". The extended family now included five children and eventually eleven grandchildren.

EPILOGUE

———◆———

BOBBY AND ROY HAD DISCUSSED their father's desire to retrace his footsteps and travel his route down the Ouachita River again. Bobby and Roy and their wives decided to do just that. They would first travel up river from Jonesville, Louisiana to Moro Bay, Arkansas and then retrace their father's nineteen twenty-two voyage on the homemade raft. They would make the voyage, not on a raft, but in a small cabin cruiser boat.

As the month of June, 2016 drew near the excitement was also growing. Everyone who had heard about the planned trip and the unusual story that encouraged and inspired the planned trip became excited. Donna had a friend from Monroe who was also in the legal profession. Bobby and Donna would always stop and have dinner with her when visiting in Louisiana. When she heard of the planned trip and the reason that had inspired the planned voyage, she quickly requested that Bobby write a story for the newspaper in Monroe and the TV stations. She notified the media about the story and they were interested in following the voyage of the two brothers and their wives.

The trip was planned for the month of June, 2016. As the planned trip drew closer, they realized that May of 2016 was a bad month on the Ouachita River. Numerous torrential rains had caused the river to rise to flood stages that had not been seen since 1929 and 1949. Memories quickly returned the two brothers to the flood of 1949 that they had experienced and many smaller floods after that. Nineteen twenty-nine was the year of all-time record floods in the central Louisiana area. Bobby and Roy had lived through some of the floods that had occurred in their lifetime. They knew that the Ouachita was sometimes unforgiving and unbiased about the number of lives it played havoc with when it flooded over its banks. In May, the Corps of Engineers for a short time closed the river to commercial traffic.

As the date for their journey neared, the rivers continued to recede and in June the voyage was on. The family always had a large family gathering in June. The family gathering that would precede the planned trip was always held the first part of June and always included family and friends from both paternal and maternal sides of the family. The planned voyage would commence following this gathering. The newspapers and television stations had contacted Bobby for a follow-up on the story and the dates for the planned voyage. The planned trip up river included a stop at a marina in Monroe and an overnight stay in Monroe. The media planned to meet the brothers at the marina to film the adventure and interview the brothers.

The plans were that Bobby and Roy would place their craft in the water in Jonesville. Advance observations of the boat ramp area did not look encouraging. The floods had caused the boat ramps to be filled with silt. The original plan to put into the water at the Jonesville Lock and Dam boat ramp was changed because of the silt and shallow water caused by the silt and debris buildup at the boat ramp.

The alternative boat ramp was to be across the Little River from Jonesville at a public boat ramp. There were problems with silt there as well. Although some of the silt and debris had been removed, there was still enough to cause problems. An attempt was made and the cabin cruiser was launched. As the brothers began their long-awaited voyage, they immediately ran into problems.

The boat engine would run great for only a short time then begin to lose power. The RPM would drop back to 1200 and would not exceed that. They returned to the boat ramp to reload the boat and determine what the problem was. They had a friend who was taking the truck and boat trailer to his home for the duration of the planned trip. He returned with the trailer and when the boat was loaded the silt prevented the truck from pulling the boat and trailer up the steep embankment. Another boater assisted in pulling the load up the hill.

Now they had to find a mechanic who would or could work on the cabin cruiser engine to determine what the problem was. It was pre-concluded that the problem had to be fuel related because the engine ran smoothly but only at a maximum of 1200 RPM.

The friend with whom Roy and Bobby were acquainted knew a man near Jena, Louisiana who was the very person they needed. This man was a diesel and engine mechanic but most importantly he worked on outboard and inboard engines. He had worked for several years as a mechanic on large tug boats running the Mississippi River and had retired after a "Turbo Charger" on a diesel engine exploded and seriously injured him. After a phone call and an explanation of the importance of the trip that they were desperately trying to begin, the mechanic said he would do the work if they could get the boat to him.

The time was slowly slipping by for the brothers to keep their planned schedule. The mechanic quickly diagnosed the problem as fuel starvation and detected that a fuel sensor switch with a breaker button had tripped. After less than an hour the problem was believed to be solved. Now the decision had to be made about beginning the trip that day with only a few hours of daylight left to navigate the Ouachita. The decision was made to delay until the next day.

The mutual friend and longtime acquaintance of Roy and his wife had retired from the Corp of Engineers. He had worked at the Columbia Lock and Dam on the Ouachita River before retirement. He suggested that they commence their trip at Columbia, Louisiana which was about midway between Jonesville and Monroe. They were only about one hour away from the Lock and Dam from the mechanic's shop. He would call the Columbia Lock and Dam supervisor and request permission for the brother's truck and boat trailer to be stored in a secure area for the duration of the trip. Permission was granted and the trip was on for the next morning. The original plans were to put the boat into the Ouachita and travel to Monroe the first day. The brothers had originally planned to be met at the Marina by several media personnel from the Monroe newspapers and the television Station. Now they needed to call the media sources and advise them of the unplanned delay. Now everything was set for the next day.

The two brothers made plans to stay at a local motel and begin the trip at 8:00 the next morning. The public boat ramp which was part of the Corps of Engineers project was just south of the Lock and Dam that the brothers would need to navigate first. The boat ramp was checked out and the silt and debris problem that they had experienced in Jonesville had been cleaned at this boat ramp so the outlook was improving. The only disappointment was that the brothers' original plans up the river from Jonesville would have taken them past several places where they had lived on the river. They were excited that they would see the old places and relive with their wives, the school boat experiences and the adventures they had had on the Ouachita River.

After a much-needed rest, the brothers and their wives arrived at the boat ramp south of the Columbia Lock and Dam at 8:00 as planned. There to meet them was the friend who had been of so much appreciated assistance. The boat was again launched into the Ouachita at a small inlet constructed by the Lock and Dam when the Corps of Engineers had constructed the Lock and Dam project at Columbia. The engine was started and was now running great. After making several short runs into the Ouachita it was determined that the fuel problem was solved and the voyage was on again.

The Corps of Engineers rules were that any vessel approaching the dam and needing to pass through would first call on the phone, the radio, or use the boat horn to advise the Lock and Dam crew that they were approaching and needed to go through the Locks. This was an adventure in itself. They had lived on or near the rivers all their life but had never been through the Lock and Dam system. There was one Lock and Dam system just south of Jonesville and one just north of Columbia. These had been constructed after the brothers had left their numerous boat adventures on the river.

When a vessel approached the Lock and Dam, they were required to remain at a safe distance from the locks until they first made contact with the crew operating the locks and then await a green signal light before approaching the locks. When the signal was given, the throttle was advanced and the boat proceeded into a large steel structure about 100' wide and about 200' long with steel sides that extended upwards about 20' above the river level. In front were large steel gates that closed off most of the water flow. When the boats entered, the steel structure the entrance gates closed and huge amounts of water was pumped into the steel structure and the water level began to rise and the boat began to rise as the level went up. When the water level in the steel structure was equal with the river on the other side of the gate, a signal was given and the front gate slowly opened to expose the river up ahead. The throttle was advanced slowly and the boat carrying the brothers and their wives was off again: destination Monroe, Louisiana Marina and then on to Moro Bay, Arkansas.

When they were safely clear of the locks, and dam, the boat speed was increased and they were off to Monroe and their first stop on their voyage to Moro Bay, Arkansas - or so they thought.

After a few minutes of smooth sailing, the engine again idled back to 1200 R.P.M. with the same problem as before. Bobby quickly opened the engine hatch and pushed the fuel switch breaker button just as the mechanic had shown him. This worked and again they were back on the river. After a couple of minutes the same problem happened again. By now the two brothers were having second thoughts.

Because of the delay, they were now hearing weather reports that severe weather was expected north of Monroe and in the southern Arkansas area just where their route would take them. With the engine problems and the weather forecasts, the brothers cancelled their trip with expectations of having the boat repaired and then rescheduling for a future date. The mechanic was called and again he said he would work on the boat to solve the fuel problem. They now knew that even if the problem was repaired they would face unknown weather challenges with the weather report. They had lived on the rivers and knew that heavy rains anywhere near the Ouachita would create problems due to the runoff. They were not willing to take the chance.

Rather than give up on the trip in its totality, the two brothers and their wives discussed the enjoyment of driving to Moro Bay and spending a few days there. They would again plan and take the boat trip in a few months when the weather was cooperating and the boat engine or fuel problem was solved. Reservations had already been made at the Moro Bay Cabins which were in the Moro Bay State Park and near the Ouachita River. The state park had a marina on the Ouachita River and this is where they were to dock the boat in their original plans. First the reservations would be confirmed. After that the television stations and news media would be notified that due to the boat fuel problems and the weather the trip had been postponed.

The mechanic assured the brothers that he could solve the problem and now that he had a few extra days he was sure the problem would be taken care of. They were now free to enjoy the next few days by jumping forward from the river voyage to a drive to their destination of Moro Bay. While there, they could visit the old sites and reminisce.

The brothers are very optimistic thinkers and not pessimists. Although the boat voyage had been planned for a long time, they were not devastated by the cancellation. Instead the trip was only delayed but there were still several days that they could have an enjoyable time. They set out to do just that.

The Johnson brothers had visited Moro Bay four years earlier when another side of the Johnsons had a family reunion there. They had visited the pavilion area but not the rest of the park. At that time, they heard of a large peach farm and fruit farm near El Dorado, so this trip would include visiting the peach farm again for some fresh fruit to take home.

Just as the weather forecasters had predicted, heavy thunder storms moved into the area and the road trip was driven in heavy downpours. When they arrived in El Dorado the weather had finally lightened up but more heavy rain was on the way. The first night was spent in El Dorado with torrential downpours during the night.

They were told of a nearby restaurant that was popular for its Cajun food. The visit was a bonus to the trip. Not only was the food excellent, but as they were eating the owner just happened to be in the restaurant and decided to come over to their table for a visit. The conversation continued and when the owner discovered that Bobby and Donna were from Austin he began an extended conversation. He informed them that he was recently in an adjoining city for a large festival they were having and he was the supplier and cook for the crawfish boil that was always popular for this festival. Donna's daughter (Bobby's step-daughter) lived in the town of Dripping Springs and had recently related that the crawfish boil was a great attraction and bonus for the festival.

During the night, the weather forecaster was again correct. Thunder storms slammed into the southern Arkansas area with a vengeance. Torrential rains persisted through the night, dumping several inches of rain on the entire area even as far south as Monroe. The brothers breathed a sigh of relief. The boat problems had been their blessing in disguise and they had not been caught on the Ouachita River during the storms nor in the aftermath of rising water and heavy debris washing down the river.

Although the rains very heavy throughout the previous day and night they were now over and the weather was great. First, they would visit the peach farm for a large supply of fresh peaches. They first visited a grocery store for several strong boxes. They would buy enough peaches to prepare for the freezer as well as eating. The farm cannot truthfully be described as a peach farm because it included a variety of fruit trees and was planted and designed so the fruit would be getting ripe over the entire spring and summer. There were peaches of several varieties, plums, blue berries and blackberries as well as other fruits.

As they drove through the area it was obvious the rains had been heavy. Thus, the history of past flooding that the brothers had experienced as they were growing up, again seemed to be following them to become a part of this narrative. Water filled the ditches and all the low-lying areas. When they were driving around the area they decided to take a route that would lead them back to Moro Bay. When they were only a few miles from Moro Bay they ran into a problem. The roads were covered with flood waters. They could see the other side and the road but Bobby and Donna knew very well the dangers of driving through flooded roads. Austin and the surrounding Hill Country were often flooded in the low water crossings and each year there were several lives lost through drowning because someone decided to risk it and try to drive through the rushing water. Thus, came the slogan "Turn Around, Don't Drown".

They would now have to return to El Dorado and take another highway to Moro Bay. This would add an additional two hours to their trip to the lodges. They discovered that they were only a few miles from the lodges when they were forced to turn around, because of the flooded highway. When they arrived at Moro Bay the evidence of heavy rain was everywhere. The State Park itself had flooding although all the roads and trails were now open. The low runoff areas were flowing to their maximum capacity.

As the brothers drove around the area of southern Arkansas they tried to locate all the areas their father had told them of when he lived in Bradley County, Arkansas. Much was left to their imagination as they tried to visualize their father's early childhood and all the tragedy and heartbreak the Johnson Clan had endured in those years prior to 1921. Then there was the construction of the raft that would eventually float them down river for over two hundred fifty miles. They hoped this mass of floating Timbers would take them down the Ouachita River to places unknown and away from the broken family, the broken past, heartbreak, and hopefully to a new life that they hoped to find.

The following is the article written for release to the news media[4].

Brothers Retrace Their Fathers
Voyage 90 Years Earlier

Bobby V. Johnson and Roy L. Johnson and their wives, left Jonesville Sunday to retrace their father's voyage from Moro Bay, Arkansas to Jonesville, La. Their voyage up the Ouachita is quite different than that of their father, Zattie's (Jack) trip in 1922. They are making the voyage in a 26-foot cabin cruiser with all the comforts of bunks, bath and galley

---

4 Appeared in Monroe News and on KNOE TV June 2016

When Jack was only a child the family began to experience hard times. In 1918 the wife and mother of seven children (plus three step-children) died shortly after giving birth to twin boys. Then six months later one of the twin boys died. Hubert Lee Johnson (Bobby and Roy's grandfather) quickly realized he could not care for the children and began to foster and adopt them out to relatives and acquaintances. Bobby and Roy's father, Jack refused to leave his father. All the other siblings were now with an older sister and relatives, with the remaining twin being adopted by another family. Then, as if the hand of fate was against them, the home that Hubert Lee had built burned to the ground. This was the last straw for Hubert Lee who had now re married.

Hubert Lee and Zattie May (Jack), who was eleven years of age, began to construct a barge or large raft out of timbers and scrap lumber. Hubert Lee's intention was to leave the area in which he was raised and had lived for most of his life and find a new area to re-establish his life. They would float down the Ouachita River until they found steady employment.

They pushed the homemade barge (raft) with their meager belongings off from the shore near Moro Bay, Arkansas in 1922 and were at the mercy of the un-predictable Ouachita, headed for parts unknown.

They landed temporarily in Monroe, Louisiana where they found work for a few weeks. Now with a few hard-earned dollars they replenished their supplies. They had been given some encouraging information about a town farther down the river, where they were told there were sawmills and cotton gins and the prospects of permanent employment. They again pushed away from shore and allowed the currents of the Ouachita to transport them to their new destination. The town was Jonesville where there were three or four sawmills operating and also a large farming and timber area.

When they arrived in Jonesville, they did indeed find employment and the prospects of beginning a new life had begun. Zattie May, who did not like his name that had been passed down for several generations, then began to go by the name of Jack and would use this name for the rest of his life. Jack, who was now twelve years of age, also began to work at one of the mills to help the family in their struggle to establish a new life in this Delta region of Louisiana. His formal education was over.

Jack's father, Hubert Lee, died in 1929 and Jack was now on his own. Jack and his stepmother did not get along. He kept in touch with his family in Arkansas who were now beginning to disperse from Arkansas to Louisiana and Alabama - everyone that is, except the twin brother who was adopted. His adoptive parents had left the Arkansas area and the Johnson family lost touch with the youngest sibling.

It would be fifty years before Jack would see his younger brother, the remaining twin, Almer. All traces of the adoptive family and brother had been lost. In 1968, Jack received word from another family member that they had just discovered that the adoptive family and brother had been living in Ft. Worth, Texas. Bobby, who was living in Lubbock, Texas and working as a civilian for the Air Force, and his wife were visiting his dad and mother in Clayton. They were given the information received about the missing brother. Bobby and his wife stopped in Ft. Worth and visited the Uncle who had heard of his siblings and only knew that there were still some family members in El Dorado, Arkansas. Contact was made and a new chapter in the life of Zattie May (Jack) Johnson would begin.

The brothers were reunited after 50 years and would continue to visit and re-establish their family ties. Almer would meet all his siblings and the new chapter began.

Jack would always desire to reverse the voyage and retrace the trip down the Ouachita River that he and his father Hubert Lee had taken when he was only eleven years of age. Bobby and Roy had continued to hope that one day they could be in a position of fulfilling their father's dream and would retrace their fathers voyage. They plan to begin their trip up the Ouachita River on Sunday June 12, with a stop at Monroe before continuing to Moro Bay, Arkansas where they plan to arrive on June 14th or 15th.

They will spend a few days at Moro Bay State Park before making their return voyage to Jonesville. The one important person missing on the long-desired voyage will be Zattie May "Jack" Johnson who died of esophageal cancer in September, 1999. Reliving all the memories and experiences of the past voyage was now, forever, only a dream. A dream, too finally be fulfilled by his sons after almost 100 years.

—◆—

CLAN-DESTINY BEGAN WITH THE PLANNED trip by boat from Jonesville, Louisiana to Moro Bay, Arkansas. The intention was to write a short description of the trip and the reason for the trip. During this trip, we planned to record notes and make a photo album which would later be published for all the family members. From this grew the book that you have just read.

In my other writings, I seem to get involved with the historical aspects of the story and find a need to include these historical records of what was happening at that time in history. I have done the same in this narrative. The purpose is to include something which is also recorded fact and is recorded in the historical records that correlate with the period in which I am writing.

I hope you have enjoyed this narrative that began with a Scottish clan, their lives in Scotland, and the centuries long turmoil that they have experienced. Our journey follows their voyage to America and centered on the family that we have traced over almost three hundred years. Their struggles were many, their accomplishments were many, and their heartache and difficulties were many as well. Yet they survive with great pride in their heritage and great pride in the country which they think is the greatest country in the world. Each member of the Johnson clan is proud of their lives in America and most of all "Proud to be an American" with Scottish heritage.

www.ingramcontent.com/pod-product-compliance
Lightning Source LLC
Chambersburg PA
CBHW060919040426
42445CB00011B/705